Gathering The Priests

For the Outpouring of
His Glory

DAN HARWELL

Copyright © 2007 by Dan Harwell

Gathering the Priests
by Dan Harwell

Printed in the United States of America

ISBN 978-1-60266-675-7

All rights reserved solely by the author. The author guarantees all contents are original and do not infringe upon the legal rights of any other person or work. No part of this book may be reproduced in any form without the permission of the author. The views expressed in this book are not necessarily those of the publisher.

Unless otherwise indicated, Bible quotations are taken from:

The Holy Bible, New International Version (NIV). Copyright © 1973, 1978, 1984, International Bible Society. Used by permission of Zondervan Bible Publishers.

The King James Version (KJV), Authorized King James Version. The New King James Version (NKJV). Copyright © 1979, 1980, 1982 by Thomas Nelson, Inc. Used by permission. All rights reserved.

www.xulonpress.com

Acknowledgements

I would like to wholeheartedly thank the following people for their vital role in the making of this book.

- First of all, I want to say thank you to my beautiful wife, Kathleen for your love, encouragement, prayer, and patience as I spent many late nights in front of the computer writing and re-writing my manuscript. I love you very much.

- Thanks to my mother in law, Cheryl Pitcairn, who diligently read and edited each chapter. You truly are a gift from God.

- Thanks to Pastor Chris Jackson, and Pastor Brent Sparks who continued to encourage me during the writing process. Your faithful support has meant a great deal to both Kathleen and I.

- Thanks to my wonderful mother, Cordelia Harwell, who has interceded for this book even before its first sentence was written. You have always been my best cheer leader. I love you mom.

- Thank you to my radical friend and hunting buddy, Bill Ouverson. Your prophetic insight has greatly blessed both my life and my ministry. I thank God everyday for your friendship.

- Thank you to my great friend and fishing buddy, Mark Nelson, who was not afraid to push me when I needed it. Finally, no more ungodly delay!

- A big Thank you to my long-time friend, Carol King. You have always been able to see the potential in me that I was unable to see. Your friendship is truly one of a kind.

- Thank you to the Madison Assembly church family who has faithfully prayed over the timing and effectiveness of this material and has helped pave the way for this book by generously covering the publishing costs.

- Thanks to the church family at Freedom Church who have also sown a great deal of prayer and support into this material. Kathleen and I will be forever knitted to you all.

Dedication

First of all I want to dedicate this book to the most important ladies in my life; my gorgeous wife, Kathleen, and our beautiful daughter, Victoria Rose. You two are my lifeline and my joy. I love you both and it is such a privilege to share each and every day with you. The Heavenly Father truly graced my life when He placed you in it.

Secondly I dedicate this book to my hero, my beloved father, Gordon Harwell, who now forever dwells in the awesome glory and presence of God. Dad, I love you and miss you and even though you are in heaven, the Godly example of your life continues to guide and impact my world.

Third, I owe such a debt to the spiritual fathers and brothers who have helped shape my character and my ministry. These wonderful leaders are: Pastor Henry Green; Glenn Phillips; Apostle Dutch Sheets;

Pastor Chris Jackson; Brent Sparks; Duane Harlow; Pastor Mark Cronauer; and Jeff Reuter. Each one of you has richly sown into my life. Your ministries have given me a foundation on which to build a ministry of my own. Over the years each of you have dedicated your time and support into my life, therefore I gladly dedicate this work to each of you.

Lastly, I dedicate this book to the King of Glory Himself, Jesus Christ. Thank You for Your unending love and mercy. Thank You for Your promises and Your guidance. Without You, I am nothing, but because of You, I am complete.

Table of Contents

✠

ACKNOWLEGEMENTS v

DEDICATION vii

INTRODUCTION xi

CHAPTER 1: *God Speaks In Code* 15

CHAPTER 2: *David's Fallen Tent* 27

CHAPTER 3: *Going After the Glory* 37

CHAPTER 4: *Called To Priesthood* 53

CHAPTER 5: *Who Do You Think You Are* 69

CHAPTER 6: *The Greatest Call of the Priest* 83

CHAPTER 7: *The Kabod and the Shekinah* 97

CHAPTER 8: *Supernatural Spiritual Hunger* ..113

CHAPTER 9: *Drilling the Wells of Glory* 121

CHAPTER 10: *The Purposes of His Glory* 131

CHAPTER 11: *Preparing For His Glory* 139

CHAPTER 12: *Truck Drivers Wanted* 149

CHAPTER 13: *Always Read the Safety Labels* ..159

CHAPTER 14: *Joining the Remnant of Priests* ..167

CHAPTER 15: *Cry for Glory* 177

Introduction

Let's Take a Journey

The Road that Leads to His Glory

What you are holding in your hand is not just a book filled with pages and words; I believe that what you are holding is actually a road map. And just like any other road map, this one has been designed to lead you on a journey. The purpose of this book is to mobilize you. My prayer is that as you read the following chapters you will begin to journey from where you are now toward a brand new destination – a destination that has the potential to radically change your life.

As you journey along, I believe that you will receive new insight into one of the primary purposes you have as a believer in Christ. There are several bends in the road ahead and at each turn you will encounter information that has the potential to challenge your previous viewpoints and paradigms. There are even a few intersections on this journey that will call for you to make a decision as to which way you are going to go.

The journey ahead is a journey of choices. You have already made the first and probably most important choice; you have opened the book and started reading. And as you read on, I believe you are positioning yourself for a brand new understanding that will minister to your life in a powerful way.

The big questions are: "What is at the end of the street? Is it just another dead end road or will I actually find something there that will change my life? Will it be worth it if I commit to the road ahead?" These are all valid questions. Let me answer them by simply saying that waiting for you at the end of this journey is a *"high calling"*. A tremendous call to ministry is waiting for you at the end of the road. This is a call to an ancient and yet extremely important office in the Kingdom of God; the office of the priest. I am not referring to the office of a liturgical clergyman. I am referring to those whose job it is to minister before the manifested Glory of God.

There is a call that is ringing out of Heaven. It is a call to gather the priests together for the next outpouring of God's glory. This call is ringing out all across the earth. The enemy is doing everything in

Gathering the Priests

his power to squelch it, but it refuses to be silenced. And all over the world, people are opening up their spirits and recognizing its sound. Those who hear it and answer the call will be the ones who will step into the office of the priest, and in doing so, will position themselves to minister before God's glory.

I invite you join me in this journey. It is a journey to an ancient and exciting place. A place filled with the manifest power of God. A place filled with signs and wonders and miracles. You may not know it yet, but you were actually created to dwell in this place. The name of this awesome place is *The Glory of God*.

When you turn the next page, our journey will begin. And as you continue to read, I pray that the Holy Spirit will come along side of you and walk with you along the path. I pray that He will awaken not only your mind and your intellect but that your soul and your spirit will also be awakened to the truth that is waiting for you along the way. I also pray that you will begin to hear and recognize the call that is ringing out from heaven. I pray that when you come to the end of this book, your journey will not come to an end, but that this book will be just the beginning. And finally, I pray that your heart will beat with passion for the manifest glory of God.

Come On! Let's go on a journey together.

Chapter One

God Speaks in Code

The 911 story that has forever changed my life

Has God ever spoken to you in code? Has He ever given you a message that seemed to make no sense at all? Have you found yourself in situations where all the details seemed to be missing and yet you knew that it was the Lord who was speaking to you? Sometimes the Lord chooses to use the circumstances and situations around us to speak to us. If you are like me, you find yourself wondering why God doesn't just come straight out with it. I have come to the conclusion that God loves to speak to us in a secret code.

Apparently, Jesus loves to speak in code as well. When Jesus taught His followers, He often used parables to illustrate a particular truth, but the odd thing is, He rarely explained the parable. He simply spoke in mysterious code and left it for the listeners to decipher the deeper meaning. It was almost as if He loved to leave people standing around scratching their heads. Why does God love to speak in code? I believe it is because something happens to us when He uses code to conceal truth. It intrigues us! It makes us wonder! It puts us on a journey for the truth. We find ourselves wanting more than anything to crack the code and find out exactly what the Lord is trying to say.

Well, about 10 years ago I found myself in that very place. I knew that The Father was trying to download a new paradigm into my spirit, but for the life of me, I was having a difficult time figuring it out.

It all started in May 1997. I was driving up the interstate in Oregon one morning, heading for work and minding my own business when a black pickup, driving way too fast, cut right in between me and the car in front of me. In fact, it nearly ran both of us off the road. I wish I could tell you that I was unaffected by this incident, and that I exhibited true Christian maturity and remained perfectly calm, but the truth is, I could instantly feel my blood rising up into my neck, as I desperately tried not to curse and use certain hand signals that are not appropriate to ministers of the Gospel. I tried to control my temper, but unfortunately my indignation got the best of me and I remember thinking to myself, "Oh yeah! I'll fix this guy". So I read his license plate number with every intention of reporting him to the authorities. The number read *"SEE 911"*. It was such an easy number to remember that I didn't even need to write it down. I decided that as soon as I got to work I would call the highway patrol and file a report. This guy was going to pay – He was going to get it for sure.

Naturally, after a cooling down period, and a short dialogue with the Lord, I began to regain control of my attitude and decided the right thing to do would be to cut the fellow a little slack, after all he was probably late for work and I have definitely been in his shoes. Oddly enough, about that time, a mini van passed me and for some reason I looked down at the van's license plate. To my surprise I discovered that it too contained the numbers 911. Another moment later I was passed again by a third vehicle having plate numbers 911. I thought to myself that it was odd to be passed three times in less than 10 minutes by vehicles having the same numbers on their license plates.

I got to work and began my day. As I busied myself I soon forgot about the black pickup and the odd number incident on the freeway. A little over an hour later I remember wondering what the time was. I wasn't wearing my watch so I looked around the office for a clock. There was a large digital clock on one of the walls that told me the time was 9:11 AM. Immediately I remembered the license plates, and wondered what the significance was with this number.

-The 911 Phenomena-

Over the next six weeks I would see this number almost every day with very few exceptions. On some days I saw it 7 or 8 times. It showed up on clocks, television adds, emergency vehicles, junk mail, more license plates, and the list goes on and on. I was literally amazed at how often I saw this number. On two occasions my grocery bill total came to exactly $9.11. This also happened once at a restaurant. Every time I saw this number it would immediately grab my attention. And to this day it still does.

At first I kept telling myself that it was only a coincidence and that sooner or later I would stop seeing it. But as it kept happening over and over, day after day, I soon came to realize that The Lord must be trying to get my attention. God was speaking in code.

"911" was the secret code that the Lord utilized to put me on a journey for truth. That six week period in 1997 was a time of intense searching for the deeper meaning. I didn't know it at the time, but what I was trying to do was "crack the code". As I searched for the answers I soon realized that my life would be forever altered by what I would discover.

-A Journey for the Truth-

I remember one Saturday afternoon while I was out shopping with some friends from church, we saw 3 cars with 911 on their plates, then we saw city bus #911, and then 4 emergency vehicles with 911 painted on their side, all less than 4 blocks from each other!

Probably the most fascinating "911" incident happened when I was out of town for the weekend. While I was gone the electricity had gone out. When I returned home the clock in my bedroom was blinking 9:11. The power had come back on exactly 9 hours and 11 minutes before I arrived home.

I began to seek the Lord for what the meaning of 911 could be. Obviously, my first conclusion was that there was an "EMERGENCY". If 9-1-1 is the number we call to report an emergency; then The Lord must be trying to tell me that there was something terribly wrong that required my attention. I searched and searched for what this emergency could be. I contacted my family members to see if anything was wrong with any of them, but none of them had anything unusual to report. I began to inquire of people at church to see if maybe the emergency was with one of them. Again I came up empty handed.

I began to wonder if the emergency had to do with me. Was I in some kind of danger? Was I sick or something? I didn't know of anything physically wrong with me that would merit an emergency situation, so I began to think that maybe this was a spiritual matter. Perhaps my spirit or my soul was in danger. I searched my heart thinking maybe I had an un-repented sin issue or an attitude that needed to be given to the Lord, but after repenting for everything I could possibly think of, the number kept appearing.

Next, I found myself wondering if the emergency had to do with a spiritual attack of the enemy. Perhaps the enemy had devised a strategy to come against me or against my ministry. So I went into spiritual warfare. I began to bind the devil. I bound him from my life, my family, my job, my ministry, my city, my state, you name it. I commanded him to leave my home, my church, my workplace, my car. Still, no change! Even after all that binding and loosing, I continued to see the number 911 - in fact it started to appear more often.

Six weeks into this ordeal, I was invited over for dinner by Jim and Chris Watson; some church friends of mine in Cottage Grove, Oregon. And for some reason I felt compelled to share with them the 911 phenomena. Chris is a mighty intercessor, and as I was sharing my story with her, she immediately heard the Lord say that 911 was a scripture from the Old Testament.

It was as if someone had hit me up side the head with a baseball bat. I had never even considered that 9:11 could be a scripture. I was so caught up with the notion that I was being warned of a pressing emergency, that it being a scripture reference had never even entered my mind. I grabbed Jim's Bible and began to search the Old Testament looking at all the Chapter 9, verse

11's that I could find. I even looked at Psalms 91:1 (which is a great scripture by the way).

I was just about to the end of the Old Testament and beginning to doubt if I was going to find it. The closing few books of the Old Testament are smaller books and many of them don't even have 9 chapters. I really thought that I must have missed it somewhere when finally I turned to Amos 9:11 and the Holy Spirit gripped me as I read these words:

In that day I will restore David's fallen tent. I will repair its broken places, restore its ruins, and build it as it used to be. (NIV)

As soon as I read that verse the Holy Spirit flooded into my spirit. He came on so suddenly and with such power that I began to weep right there in Jim and Chris' living room. I immediately knew that this was what 911 had been about the last six weeks. Then the Lord reminded me of something that had happened more than six months earlier. He reminded me that several months before the 911 phenomena had even begun; the Lord had already given me this verse.

-Forgotten Direction-

One Sunday Morning, back in November of 1996, as I was preparing for the morning worship service at our church, the Lord impressed upon me the word "restoration". As the Minister of Music for our church, I thought that the Lord was trying to give me a direction for the morning worship service so I picked up my concordance and began to search for scriptures with the words "restore" or "restoration" in them. The Lord led me to Amos 9:11.

As I read the verse that morning I heard the voice of the Lord say;

"The form of worship and the exposure of my glory that was available in David's Tent is the form of worship and glory that I will bless and restore to the earth in this generation."

I really didn't understand what this meant, I admit, I knew very little about "David's tent". I was running late that Sunday morning, and I knew that I wouldn't have time to research the meaning of this scripture; so I wrote down the word that the Lord given me, then highlighted the verse in my Bible, and told myself to study it later. Then I headed off for worship practice and pre-service prayer. At the time, I was convinced that the Lord was trying to speak to me, but as time passed and busyness set in, I forgot all about Amos 9:11, and the message that the Lord had given me.

Now, however, several months later, as I sat in Chris and Jim's living room, I clearly remembered the Word the Lord had spoken. The Father now had my full attention. I wasn't sure why He decided to use license plates, clocks and grocery store receipts to get my attention, but I was convinced that He definitely had a purpose for all this. I was filled with anticipation as I realized that the Lord was about to reveal to me a truth that I had not known before. And I was ready to learn all I could about Amos 9:11.

-No walls-

I began to pray, study the Word, and read what other authors had said regarding this verse. As I studied, I realized that Amos wasn't referring to the home or living quarters of David, he was referring to the temporary tabernacle that David had pitched to hold the Ark of the Covenant. David's desire was to build a glorious temple to house the Ark, but God had told him that his son would be the one to build the temple. Until then, the Ark would need a place to rest where people could worship the Lord, so David pitched a tent.

As I continued to study, The Lord gave me an incredible passion for the restoration of the Tabernacle of David. I wanted desperately to learn all that I could about the subject. As I poured over what other authors and Bible scholars had to say about David's tabernacle, I came across a fascinating study that has gripped my heart and has changed my life in a powerful way. It was as if this revelation was simply waiting for me to come by and pick it up.

The study suggested that David's tabernacle was a tabernacle without walls. The study continued to explain that it was possibly a simple, open sided, merchants tent. The Hebrew word used to describe David's tent is *cukkah,* and one of its definitions is: *an open sided merchant's tent.* Merchants used these tents to sell their goods and wares in an open market area. If this was the case with David's tabernacle, then David's tent would have had no walls. Anyone passing by the tent, Jew or Gentile alike could look in and see the Ark of the Lord and the flame of His Glory that rested between the cherubim. As I studied this possibility I began to pray and ask the Lord to confirm this. He took me to Psalms 63:2 where David, even though he was not a priest, boasts of seeing The Lord's glory in the sanctuary. Then, a few years later, Tommy Tenney's book, *"God's Favorite House"* was released, and in his book, Tommy Tenney shares the same conclusion that David's tent was an open sided tabernacle.

The Lord began to reveal to me the meaning of the prophetic words He had given to me when I first read this verse. The exposure of His glory that He wants to bless and re-establish to this generation is one that is visible to both believers and non-believers. He wants to restore His rightful place in the midst of His people. He longs for worship that has no walls. No longer will His glory be limited to a few Levitical priests. In David's Tent, everyone, even the Gentiles could look in and see the glory of God resting upon the Ark.

-It's All About His Glory-

I tell you the truth, The Father is about to unleash His glory once again upon the earth. For too many years, the church has tried to tell God "how", "when", and "where" He can move in our midst. We have attempted to dictate the presence of the Lord. We have tried to set the timing of revival. But now the Lord will set the precedence on His glory and His presence. His glory will no longer be held back by man's meaningless agendas and boundaries. He is tearing down veils and removing walls of religion. God is breaking out.

-Sept. 11th, 2001-

As you have read this chapter, you are probably reminded of another significant "911". That of course in regards to the attack on the World Trade Center on September, 11, 2001. Just like everyone else, I was really shaken by what happened that September morning. Not only was I shocked by the tragedy but I was also shaken by the date on which it fell. You may remember that after the attack many of the news organizations referred to it as "9 11" instead of "Sept. 11". For several weeks, everywhere you looked, you saw the numbers 9 11. I do not believe that this was simply coincidental. Interestingly, since 2001 there has been a new emphasis in the body of Christ regarding the coming glory of God. An enormous amount of songs, messages, and articles about the Glory of God have been released into the body of Christ since 2001. Prophets are prophetically speaking about God's glory. Apostles, Pastors and Evangelists are preaching and teaching about God's glory. Psalmist and song writers are writing music regarding the Glory of God. Intercessors are crying out for more of The Father's manifest glory. Something is happening in the Spirit realm.

As I have continued to read and listen to what the prophets and the authors are saying, I believe they are confirming over and over that Amos 9:11 has indeed begun to be fulfilled in our generation. God has begun to restore the Tabernacle of David.

Our Heavenly Father is ready to visit the earth with His glory in an even greater way than He did in the tabernacles of old. He is looking for the people and the places that are ready to receive what He has to pour out. He is looking for people He can trust with His "Manifest Presence".

He is re-pitching David's Tent and once again it will be void of all the walls and veils of religion. His desire is for His glory to be completely visible to both the believer and the non-believer alike. We are living in the day spoken of by the prophet Amos. God Almighty is about to visibly expose Himself to the earth. A new visitation of His presence is coming and we will see it established in this generation.

Chapter Two

David's Fallen Tent

Rebuilding the Tabernacle of His Glory

When you compare the three tabernacles of the Old Testament you may find it difficult to believe that David's tent is the one that God has chosen to restore to our generation. You can't help but wonder why God wouldn't want to restore Moses' tabernacle or the temple of Solomon instead. After all, Moses' tabernacle was the first tabernacle; it was there that The Lord's presence first came to dwell among His chosen people. Or Solomon's temple, with all its beauty and splendor, would seem like the obvious choice. Solomon's temple was so enormous that the outer courts alone could accommodate thousands of worshipers at once. So why choose David's tent? In Man's eyes, this little tent is by far the least of the three tabernacles.

David's tent did not have the fine linens and furnishings of Moses' tabernacle, nor did it hold the beauty and size of Solomon's temple. In fact it can hardly be called a tabernacle. It is only considered one because it housed the Ark of The Lord for a season. Yet it is David's tent that the prophet Amos said would be repaired, restored and rebuilt.

-Access to His Glory-

David's tent had no walls, no seamless veil and no outer or inner courts. It was merely a tarp stretched out overhead and suspended by poles to shield the Ark from the weather. So why did God bless this place? I believe the reason God blessed David's tent was because of what it represented. Access!

The Father wants us to have access to Him. In fact, the original purpose of the Ark of the Covenant was to provide a physical location where God's glory could dwell among His people. He wasn't satisfied ruling over the earth from a distant Heaven; therefore, He had to have an earthly throne where His people could have access to Him. When Moses constructed the Ark of the Covenant, he fashioned it to represent The Father's throne in Heaven. He was literally constructing an earthly throne for the Glory of God. The desire of Father's heart has always been for His glory to dwell in the midst of His beloved.

This is still the desire of Father's heart today. We are the passion of His heart. He longs to commune with us. His love for us is like a Father's love for His children or a Groom's love for His bride. God desires us! So often, we fail to see God the Father as someone who is passionately in love with us. Unfortunately, our view of God is usually limited to an authoritative figure, and though it is true, He is the Final Authority over the entire universe, yet this Almighty Master has a driving passion in His heart. The truth is the very passion of Heaven itself is focused toward you and me. We are God's prized creation.

I believe the reason The Lord blessed David's tent was because of the fact that it had *"no walls"*. For the first time since the fall of mankind, anyone, whether they were Jews or Gentiles, had visual access to the glory of God. His glory was on display for all to see. I believe that is why the prophet Amos foretold the re-establishing of David's tent. The Lord wants to be visible once again.

-A Veil of Flesh and Bone-

David's tent broke the rules. In both Moses' tabernacle and Solomon's temple there was a heavy veil that separated the Ark from the worshipers. This was mandated by The Lord to protect the worshipers. God's holiness always accompanied His glory, and God knew that sinful man could not stand in the presence of His holiness and live; therefore a heavy veil was placed in front of the Ark.

So how did David get away without putting up walls or veils in his tent? He broke the rules and yet it seems as if he got away with it. Actually he didn't get away with it. David's tent did have a veil, but it was not made of heavy linen, instead it was made up of Flesh and Bone. The Levitical priests became the veil. They were to sanctify themselves and stand around the Ark of the Covenant day and night and worship the Lord. David wrote about them:

Psalms 134:1 says:

"Behold, Bless ye the Lord, all ye servants of the Lord which stand by night in the house of the Lord......" (KJV)

Somehow David got away with replacing a linen veil with a human one and The Lord blessed it. The Bible tells us that David was "A man after God's own heart", and he knew that the passion of The Father's heart was to dwell among His people. So, he took a chance. He told the Levitical priests to sanctify and purify themselves, and to minister before the Ark. The priests became the veil. They worshiped with their singing, their instruments, and their dancing - and the Lord blessed it. They worked in shifts one group of priests being relieved by another so that there was a constant uplifting of intercession and worship to the Lord before the Ark of the Covenant.

Interestingly, this model of worship and intercession has been reinstated back to the body of Christ through "Harp and Bowl" style intercessory worship. God is in the process of restoring the very worship style of David's tent all over the world. He is not merely restoring this worship style so that we can have another option for Sunday morning; He is restoring it because it holds an important key to the global revival ahead of us. The Lord is presently raising up intercessory prayer houses around the world that are implementing the Harp and Bowl worship model. The incense of intercession mixed with the sounds of pure worship is rising up before the Lord in this hour from all over the earth. In several of these prayer houses the worship never stops, it is constant just like at David's tent.

As was already stated, in David's tent, the priests would work in shifts, one group of priests replacing another group so that the Ark continually and constantly had live worship and intercession surrounding it. The priests became the veil surrounding the earthly throne of God. Unlike a heavy linen veil, this human veil did not completely conceal the Ark. Any one passing by could look between the worshipers and see the actual flame of the glory of God resting upon it. The glory of God was visible to all, regardless of their history or their sin, The Father made Himself visible to all.

-The Father is making Himself Visible Again-

I believe that God wants that kind of visibility again in our generation. The church today tries to keep God's presence inside of our impressive buildings and well planned programs. In a way, we have built a wall or a veil around the presence of The Lord. We don't want just anyone looking in too closely, because we are not sure what they will think about us. We try to keep great outpourings of The Lord to a minimum because we don't want God ruining our reputation. We have become more concerned with pleasing man than pleasing Our Heavenly Father.

God will no longer be held behind walls built by man. He is tired of people walking right pass His presence and not even knowing He's there. God is longing for more visibility. He longs for His glory to be made known in all the earth. We have built heavy veils around The Lord's presence. They are not made of heavy linen or walls of stone; they are made of man's religiosity.

Isaiah 29:13 says:

"The Lord says; these people come near to Me with their mouths and honor Me with their lips, but their hearts are far from Me. Their worship of Me is made up only of rules taught by men."(NIV)

According to this verse, religiosity (rules taught by men), is what causes the hearts of man to be "far from God". Religious rules were formed to keep things in order and keep things manageable. They were supposed to keep us from getting out of control or getting out of line, but too often all that they have accomplished is holding back God's glory. Religion tries to tell us how to sing right, how to pray right, and how to say all the right things, but according to Isaiah 29 these things are usually just *lip service*. Unfortunately, religiosity does not teach our hearts how to draw near to God, in fact, if we are not careful, religion will sometimes push our hearts far away from God. The Lord clearly wants to tear down the walls and veils of man's religiosity. He wants more visibility. He is ready to make His glory known on the earth again.

Often, when we think about the glory of God, our minds wander off to the heavens where we envision The Heavenly Father sitting on His throne surrounded by worshiping angels. We often find it difficult to think that the glory of God would actually come and inhabit space here on earth. Yes, the glory of God resides around His throne, but the desire of Father's heart is for His glory to dwell here in the midst of His people. The Lord is searching for locations where He can restore David's tent. He is also looking for priests that He can trust with His manifest presence. He wants true worshipers who will stand by night in the house of the Lord but not block out His glory from those passing by.

-Now is the Time! - We are the People!-

I believe that we are living in the time that was spoken of in Amos 9:11. If you read the rest of the chapter you see that Amos also prophesies that in that same time Israel would be planted back into her promised land never to be uprooted again. On May 14, 1948, Israel took back control of her land and declared her independence as a nation. Then in June of 1967, in what is now called the "Six Day War", Israel secured the city of Jerusalem and the areas surrounding it. Since that time the descendants of Abraham have been relocating to Israel every year. In fact, in the last 10 years alone we have seen large numbers of Jews returning to the land of their forefathers. The season that Amos 9 speaks of is now.

God is looking for some David's. He is searching for a people who will take a chance. He wants a "Man or Woman after His own Heart" who understands His passion for His people. Someone who will break away from what religion and tradition tells them to do and begin to do what The Father's heart says to do.

David knew that the passion of Father's heart was to dwell among His people. He knew this when he pitched his tent. He knew this when he went after the Ark. He knew this when he ordered the priests to stand around it and worship. He also knew that this wasn't the way his forefathers worshipped. He knew that his tabernacle did not look like the tabernacle of Moses. But that didn't matter because David knew the heart of God. And instead of following tradition, he chose to follow the desires of God's heart.

-The Tent of Restoration-

The tent of David not only speaks of access, it also speaks of restoration. The Ark of the Lord was once again brought back and restored to the people of the Lord; for it had been away for twenty years. The Ark of the Lord had been forgotten. More than twenty years before David became king, the Philistines had stolen the Ark. They kept it for seven months and then returned it to Israel's border. It was brought to a border town; the Gibeonite city of *Kirjath Jearim*, where it waited for the priests and rulers to come and get it. But the rulers never came. According to I Samuel 7, it waited there for twenty years. The glory of God had been neglected and rejected by the leadership of Israel. The Bible says that during the entire reign of King Saul the Ark was not even inquired of.

When David brought the Ark of the Covenant into Jerusalem, he wasn't just bringing back an artifact or a piece of religious furniture; he was restoring the manifest glory of God back to its rightful place in the midst of the people. The tent of David became the tent of restoration. It became the place where The Lord once again tabernacled with His people.

Have you ever been guilty of saying, "I'm just waiting on God?" People may ask you how your ministry is going and you say, "I am just waiting on the Lord to show me the next step to take". So often we can confuse ourselves by thinking we are in God's waiting room when in fact God is in our border town.

David could have said, *Lord, You know we really need a fresh visitation of Your glory, so Lord I am just going to wait on You to move on our behalf. I'm just going to sit here and wait, and when You get good and ready, then You go ahead and move, OK God?!*

If David would have prayed a prayer like that he would still be waiting. The reason why David didn't pray such a foolish prayer was because he knew that The Lord had already sent His manifest glory to the earth, and that it was resting between two cherubim on top of the Ark of the Lord in Israel's border town. David knew the Ark was not going to transport itself to Jerusalem, if he wanted God's glory; he was going to have to go and get it. So often we believe that we are waiting on The Lord when in reality The Lord is waiting on us.

I believe God is ready to release His glory in the earth today and one of the reasons He hasn't done it yet is because no one has gone after it. No one wants to prepare a place for it. Just like David, if we want God's holy habitation we are going to have to go after it with all our hearts.

Chapter Three

Going After the Glory

Taking the Glory of God to the People of God

Have you ever wondered why The Lord gave David the title *"Man after His own heart?"* What was it about David that so moved the heart of The Father that he came away with such awesome credentials? I believe the reason David received this famous distinction was because David had a passion for the presence of the Lord. As a passionate worshiper, he was no stranger to the Lord's presence. One of David's greatest accomplishments was that he was the King who brought back the glory of God.

David knew as a young child that The Lord had a plan for His life. He did not come to this conclusion because he belonged to a wealthy family or because he was the heir to a position of great honor and riches. In fact, David knew that if he relied on his position as the son of Jesse, he wasn't going to get very far. He was the youngest son in a large family with many older brothers. In the Hebrew culture this meant that he was the least in his family. He knew that the greatest portion of his father's inheritance would fall to the eldest brothers and his portion would be meager at best. Yet as a young shepherd boy, tending his father's sheep, David discovered a strength that surpassed his own.

-Worshiper First, King Second-

At a very young age David had a passion to worship the Lord. As a skilled musician, he would sing, dance, and write psalms of worship to the God of Abraham, Isaac and Jacob. While spending time in worship and adoration before the Lord, David tapped into something he knew was greater than any inheritance his earthly father had to offer.

As a young worshiper, David discovered that there was an amazing power and strength that accompanied the presence of the Lord. David spent a great deal of time simply abiding with The Father. As evident in the many Psalms that he wrote, the Lord taught David many valuable truths regarding His presence and His glory.

Because of David's faithfulness, God bestowed on him great abilities. As David learned to move in the power of the Lord, he was given the strength to single-handedly kill a lion, a bear, and the giant Goliath. The Lord also gave him the ability to worship God in Saul's court and secretly drive out demons. Regardless of the fact that he was the least in his family, David knew that The Lord had a plan for his life. He knew that the Lord would use him in a mighty way. Of course as you already know, through an amazing turn of events, God stripped the mantle of kingship from the lineage of Saul and gave it to David.

What happens when a true worshiper of God becomes the leader of a nation? The Lord's presence is held as the highest priority in the land. David's first line of business as the new king of Israel was to bring back the glory of God. His desire was to get as close to God's glory as he could; so he determined to go after it.

David made two attempts to bring God's glory back to Jerusalem. The first one failed miserably, and after David licked his wounds and learned his lessons, he tried again. The second attempt proved victorious.

There are several important lessons you and I can learn from David's first and second attempts to bring back the Ark of the Lord. As we study this story we can easily see a picture of our modern day church. In many ways the church today actually parallels this story. If we do a little comparing we can see how many times in the recent history of the church, our attempts to host a revival or to see God's glory released in the earth, look a whole lot like David's *first* attempt to go after the Ark. In the same way, I believe that as we apply the principles of David's *second* attempt, we will see God's release of glory in our day.

-Good Plan vs. God's Plan-

In 2 Samuel 6 we read about David's first attempt at bringing the Ark of the Lord back from Abinadab's house in Kirjath Jearim to the city of Jerusalem. The Bible doesn't give us all the details that were happening, but from the scripture you can see that David wanted everything to be just right. He probably pulled together the religious leaders of the day and came up with the best possible plan. They would contract the nation's finest carpenters to build them a beautiful cart that would carry the Ark of the Covenant. They would call on Israel's most skilled musicians to play their harps, psalteries, timbrels, cornets, and cymbals. They would invite the entire nation to come and witness the event. There would be dancing and singing and praising the Lord the entire journey from the border town to the capital city. There would be a great feast waiting for them back in Jerusalem when they arrived with the Ark of the Lord. What a celebration it was going to be!

So the day came for the Ark to be brought up from Abinadab's house and all the people had assembled together. Abinadab and his family had lived with the Ark in their home for the past 20 years, so his two sons, Ahio and Uzzah, would go before and behind the Ark and sort of look after it. You know the story! Everything was going according to plan until they came to Nachan's threshing floor. Here at the threshing floor the cart hit a bump and the Ark began to teeter. Not wanting the Ark to fall off the cart, Uzzah quickly reached up to steady the Ark and when he did God's anger burned toward Uzzah and God struck him dead.

All of a sudden the celebration took a sour turn. The people were now fearful of the Ark and not sure if they were ready to embrace it. David wasn't so sure either. He said in 2 Sam. 6:9, "How shall the Ark of the Lord come to me?" David realized that the holiness of God accompanied the glory of God and he wasn't sure if Israel was ready for God's holiness. So here at Nachan's threshing floor the first attempt came to an end.

David's motive was right. He wanted this to be a big deal, full of fanfare and awe. The reason for the fanfare was because he wanted the Lord to be honored and pleased, and He also wanted the entire nation to see the worth and the importance that the Ark was to the king of Israel. He wanted to send a message that said God's glory will once again be held in high esteem. The problem wasn't that David's heart was wrong; the problem was David had not searched for The Father's heart. The Father had already set precedence for transporting His glory.

Too many times we try and help God out by doing things that seem noble to us. There are times when God will honor our noble attempts, but when it comes to His glory we must search for The Father's heart.

Today's church too often resembles David's cart. We try to come up with the best programs and religious acts that will move the hand of God. We will pull together our best people and try to strategize how we can get the best results. We will even appoint people to look after the glory like Ahio and Uzzah just in case something doesn't go according to plan. There is nothing wrong with strategizing, but we must be sure that we have the heart of The Father and the mind of Christ before we go and build the cart.

Too many times we leave God outside the board room when we are making plans regarding His presence. When we do this we can be assured that The Lord will turn over our apple cart every time. When it comes to His presence and His glory, He already has a plan. It is not necessary to come up with a new one; we simply need to find out what His plan is.

David went away from Nachan's threshing floor not sure of what to do next. He was disappointed with God. He was disappointed with himself. And he was embarrassed of what had just happened in front of the entire nation.

As David was reflecting on what his next step should be, the Ark was moved to the nearby home of Obed-Edom. After what happened to Uzzah, Obed-Edom made sure that the holiness of God was respected. He did not allow anyone to touch the Ark or defile it in any way. The Lord brought great prosperity to Obed-Edom and all he possessed because of the way he handled the glory of God.

-Going after God, God's Way!-

When David heard of the prosperity the Ark was bringing Obed-Edom, he determined once again to bring it to Jerusalem where it could dwell in the midst of the people of God. So, David began to study past moves of God. He began to ask himself, Just how did Moses move this thing around? As David studied the Mosaic Law regarding the Ark of the Covenant he discovered something that was missing in his first attempt; the Levitical Priests! To do this correctly it was going to take Levitical priests. So once again David began to prepare to go after the glory of God.

Meanwhile, Obed-Edom heard that David was intending on coming back for the Ark, therefore, he also found himself in a preparation time. He was about to make a decision that would alter his life as he knew it. Ever since the Ark came to Obed-Edom's home his life was blessed enormously. Not only were his crops, livestock, and finances blessed, but I believe that something happened to the man himself. In the short months that Obed-Edom cared for the Ark, he made a very important and valuable discovery; the manifest glory of God accompanied the Ark.

-God's glory will change your life-

Obed-Edom had the luxury of spending the past few months literally living and dwelling in the manifest presence and glory of God. This encounter with God's glory impacted Obed-Edom in a mighty way. As you study his life you find that he made a huge shift due to this encounter with God's glory. The Bible tells us that after David came and took the Ark of the Covenant to Jerusalem that Obed-Edom moved to Jerusalem as well. In fact, the Bible records Obed-Edom as one of the gate keepers to David's tabernacle. Obed-Edom's life was so impacted by the glory of God that nothing else mattered to him anymore. The glory of God would become his life. He walked away from his land holdings in a season where everything was blessed and going very well. He literally gave it all up so that he could remain in the manifest glory of God. From Obed-Edom's story we can see how The Lord's manifested glory has the power to change your value system. The things that seem important to you now may radically change as you are impacted by the fullness of His manifest glory.

In 2 Samuel 6:12-19, and In 1 Chronicles 15, we read about David's second attempt to bring the Ark to Jerusalem. This time he knew the heart of The Father and he was ready to do it God's way. He gathered together the Levites and the priests and told them to sanctify and set themselves apart. They were to consecrate themselves. The priests would carry the Ark on their shoulders as in the days of Moses.

-Sacrificial Worship-

So they went to the home of Obed-Edom and began the journey to Jerusalem. The Bible tells us that when they had gone only six paces, David stopped the parade and sacrificed oxen and sheep before the Lord. This was not going to be the flashy, crowd pleasing journey they had first planned. This would be a bloody, sweaty, God pleasing journey.

When they had finally reached Jerusalem, David stripped off his kingly robes, and dressed only in a linen ephod, he humbly danced before the Lord. He did not worship as the king of Israel; He worshiped as the servant of the Most High God. The glory of the Lord was once again in the midst of His people.

David was praised by all of Israel, The entire nation rejoiced with the king over the return of the Ark of the Lord. David's success at bringing back the glory of God to Jerusalem paints a prophetic picture for believers today. The revelations that David discovered as he prepared to try again are in many ways the same revelations that we must realize if we want to see The Lord release His glory upon us.

The most important thing that David did the second time around was he studied the past moves of God. David not only looked to see how the Ark was transported in history, but he also studied what The Lord had said in regards to how to properly handle His glory. David remembered what the Levitical Priests were for. God had a chosen, anointed people whose main purpose was to minister before His glory. It is interesting when you stop and think about those Levites. They were to minister before the Ark, that was their highest calling; yet for 20 years the Ark of the Lord was sitting in a border town; everyone knew it was there, and yet no one went after it. The men who were chosen to minister before it hadn't even seen it in over 20 years.

These men hadn't kept themselves pure and righteous as they were supposed to. They had grown cold and callous in their beliefs. Some of the younger ones may not have even been circumcised. They still practiced their religious rites and rituals, but there was no longer any fear of the Lord to keep themselves sanctified and set apart because the glory of God was no longer in their midst.

-Restoring your Destiny-

So, how are a bunch of calloused, hard hearted, rebellious, possibly uncircumcised priests supposed to carry God's glory when they hadn't even seen it in over 20 years? The Bible tells us that they simply consecrated themselves. They repented of their callousness and purified themselves. They returned to the Levitical code that had been handed down from the priests before them.

This is such an awesome picture for us. Many Christians today have the call of God on their lives, and they know without a shadow of doubt that The Lord has chosen them to fulfill a specific calling. Yet they have allowed life and all its busyness to derail their dreams and push back their destiny. For some Christians, perhaps it has been 20 years since the passion for the purposes of God has burned inside of them. Well, guess what? It isn't too late! The Levitical call still stands. It's never too late to repent and sanctify yourself. Old dreams can be resurrected. The Father longs to breathe new life back into your hopes and callings.

-Sacrifice Always Accompanies God's Glory-

As we take a deeper look at David's journey from Obed-Edom's home to Jerusalem, we see it as a sacrificial journey. It is a journey filled with death. They had only gone six paces, barely outside of the house of Obed-Edom, when David commanded them to stop, build an altar, and sacrifice both oxen and sheep to the Lord. Although the Bible does not state this, some Bible scholars believe that David stopped and sacrificed every 6 paces on his journey to Jerusalem. If this was the case, then there would have been a string of altars 6 paces apart from Obed-Edom's house to Jerusalem. You could still smell the burning flesh from the previous sacrifice as you were preparing for the next one. Regardless if this was the case or not, one thing is clear, David made certain that sacrifice was a big part of this journey.

There is always a price to pay for the glory of God. Sacrifice has always accompanied new moves of His presence. There is always sweat, blood and tears involved in birthing these new moves of the Spirit. So often we want to get around the price tag. We want to reap the benefit without paying the price. The Bible tells us to count the cost. If we truly want to embrace the glory of God, we must also embrace the cost.

-Pushing Past the Opposition-

After David reached Jerusalem he ran into yet another battle before finishing his journey. This last battle was with opposition. There seems to always be those who will stand up against any true move of God. But this opposition did not come from some fringe person that chose to simply disagree with everyone else; this opposition came from his very wife. Michal was the daughter of King Saul. If you remember, King Saul didn't even inquire of the Ark during his entire rule. Now, here his daughter is the only recorded negative voice that lifts a complaint against bringing back the glory of God.

Michal was not pleased with the actions of her husband. She criticized him for his behavior in front of the nation. She said that David was being undignified and not acting in a kingly manner. I love David's response to this accusation:

In 2 Samuel 6:22 David says,

"I will become even more undignified than this" (NIV)

David refused to be held back by some traditional, religious, legalistic queen that said he had to act or look a certain way. His only concern was in pleasing The Father. He could care less how he appeared in the eyes of man; he only cared how he appeared to the eyes of the Lord.

There is a valuable lesson to be found in David's response to Michal's complaint. Why did David strip down and dance practically naked before the Lord? In the eyes of man this was an extremely foolish gesture. There does not seem to be much wisdom in a spiritual or political leader to act in such a ridiculous manner. However, all through scripture we see that The Lord frequently used the foolish and absurd things to accomplish his will.

I Corinthians 1:27 says:

"God has chosen the foolish things of the world to put to shame the wise, and God has chosen the weak things of the world to put to shame the things which are mighty." (NKJV)

As you attempt to restore the manifest glory of God in your home or fellowship, let me assure you that you may be asked by the Lord to do what could be termed as *"the foolish things"*. And if you are obedient and do these peculiar things, I guarantee that you will run into opposition, possibly from people you consider key individuals in your lives. If you are like most people, your natural instinct will be to try and work out a compromise to make everyone happy.

No one wants to ruffle the feathers of their friends, family, or leaders, so they make minor adjustments until everyone can agree. However, if you are not careful you can adjust and adjust until you are no longer going in the same direction that God intended on you to go. If an airplane pilot set the direction of his plane just a degree or two off course, and stayed that way for several hours, eventually he would be hundreds of miles from his original destination. We must be careful that we are not so influenced by those around us that we alter from our God given calls and destinies. Compromise even in the slightest manner can have huge impacts on the goals and visions that The Lord has for us.

Oh, thank the Lord, David didn't do that. He didn't care that the Highfalutin', grandiose, honorable queen of Israel had an objection. He knew the heart of The Father and would not be derailed from reaching the goal set out in front of him. He wanted to be a God pleaser more than a man pleaser, and if that meant looking undignified or foolish than so be it. So he pressed past the present opposition and kept his focus on the purpose before Him; restoring God's manifest glory to its rightful place.

-Well Worth the Cost-

David's second attempt to bring back the Ark was extremely successful. Was it expensive? You bet it was! It came with a hefty price tag. Ah, but it was well worth it. David successfully brought the manifest glory of God into the midst of the people once again, and in doing so he began a restoration of the relationship between the children of Israel and Father God.

The Father's manifested glory is indeed coming to the earth again. But there is a price tag that must be paid. As God's chosen priests we must consecrate ourselves. We must purify our hearts and humble ourselves, even if it requires being a little foolish or undignified. Some of us may need our hearts circumcised. We may need to cut certain things out of our lives that must go if we are to be carriers of the Lord's glory.

We also must prepare a place for His glory. We must be willing to sacrifice every step of the way if needed to see God's glory released in our midst. We will meet opposition, you can count on that; maybe even from people we love and are close to. But regardless of the opposition, we must long to be men and women after God's own heart that will put His desires over the desires of men. We must join His holy priesthood.

Is The Father's manifest glory waiting in our border town? I think that it is indeed. And I believe that He is looking for a holy priesthood who will go after His glory and sacrificially pay the price to see it released in the earth. I believe God is gathering the priests.

Chapter Four

Called to Priesthood

The Process of Becoming a Conduit of God's Glory

Almost every one of us at one time or another has attempted to cook something while following a recipe. As we all know, we must have all the ingredients if we are to be successful. There are some recipes that give you optional ingredients that can be left out or substituted, but in every recipe there are mandatory, key ingredients that are critically important in order for the recipe to work.

When it comes to re-building David's tent and restoring the glory of God to the earth there is a divine recipe that must be followed. The problem for us, however, is The Lord hasn't given us all the ingredients up front. Instead, He tells us only which ingredients are needed right now, and as we are faithful to blend those together properly then He will tell us what we are going to need next.

One of the mandatory ingredients required for restoring God's glory is priests. God needs a holy priesthood prepared and ready before He will pour out His next wave of glory on the earth. After all, it was the priests who stood around David's tent and ministered to the Lord in the beauty of His holiness; and it was the priests who sacrificially went after the glory and re-established the Ark to its rightful place in the midst of the people.

Wanted: Priests

I believe that The Lord is currently in the priest hiring business. He has His "Help Wanted" sign out and is waiting for you and me to come in and fill out an application of employment. So what does it take to qualify for the position of priesthood? To find that out we need to look at the priestly Levitical code that God gave to Moses. This Levitical order shows us exactly what was required by the Levites in order to be priests unto the Lord. We may not live under the Old Testament Law any longer, but the requirements for priesthood are in many ways still the same today.

Exodus 29 tells the story of Aaron and his sons being consecrated to the Lord as priests. They were to be the first men to serve Israel in the priestly office. The process that was used to prepare them for priesthood would be passed down through the generations to the future priests of Israel.

As you read this chapter you see a procession that takes place for Aaron and his sons. In verse 4, we read that Moses took them to the entrance of the tabernacle. Here, just outside the tabernacle, they were prepared for service. First they were stripped of their old garments. No articles of clothing were left on the priests. Their outer garments, their under garments, as well as their head coverings were removed. Not only were they stripped of their old garments but they were also stripped outside the tabernacle in the open where they were exposed before all of Israel.

As the process continued, the priests were next washed from head to toe with water. No part was left unwashed. Exodus 29 tells us that Moses washed them. They were not even allowed to wash themselves. How embarrassing this must have been. They were not allowed to put on the new priestly garments until they were completely clean.

After they were bathed in water, then Moses redressed them in their priestly garments. They were dressed in a Tunic, a Robe, and an Ephod. We will look at these garments in more detail later in this chapter.

After their bodies were clothed in the new garments, then Moses took a mitre (or Turban) and placed it on their heads. He then placed a crown on top of the mitre.

Once all their garments were in place then Moses began the anointing ceremony. The first anointing was an anointing of blood. Fresh blood was placed on the right earlobes, right thumbs, and right big toes of the priests. After this came a second anointing of both blood and oil. The blood and the oil was mingled together and sprinkled all over the new outer garments of the priests.

Following the ceremony, the priests were permitted to enter the tabernacle, but they were not allowed to begin their duties. They were to wait inside the tabernacle for seven days. They were not permitted to leave or to commence their duties until after the seven day period.

-The Process-

You may be asking yourself, "How does this relate to us today? Do we have to go through this same process?" I believe the correct response to that question is in fact, yes! The process that the priests of old went through in the natural shows us what we should expect to go through in the spiritual. Exodus 29 draws a spiritual roadmap for us. This map shows us the journey the Lord will take us on in order to prepare us to be modern day priests. Let's look at these steps one at a time and observe the significance each of them hold for us today.

First, we see that the priests were brought to the entrance of the tabernacle but not allowed to enter.

They were taken to the outer courts of the tabernacle. The outer courts are often referred to as the courts of praise. For us today, I believe this is symbolic of the drawing of the Holy Spirit. It is often through worship and praise that that Holy Spirit draws us into His presence. He brings us to His outer courts of worship where he begins to prepare us for service. As priests, we must be men and women of worship. We should allow ourselves to be taken away into times of communion with Him. It is here that He is able to prepare us for priesthood.

In the past 20 years there has been an unprecedented increase in the area of worship in the church. There have been more books written, more albums recorded, and more conferences given on praise and worship in the past few years than there has ever been in the entire known history of the church. I believe that The Father is in the process of wooing us by His Spirit to the outer courts of praise where He can prepare us for the move of His glory that is coming to the earth.

Next, comes the stripping process! If we are to be priests before the glory of God, we should expect to be stripped. The Lord must remove our old garments if He is going to give us new ones. The Lord wants to array us in robes of righteousness, and the Bible says that our own righteousness is as filthy rags. The Lord will first help us out of our filthy rags that we believe are righteous, so that He can give us the new robes of His true righteousness.

Sometimes the Lord will strip away the things that we hold dear and are valuable in our eyes, so that He can replace them with new things that He holds dear. Even before becoming priests, Aaron and his sons were already a part of the leadership of Israel. As leaders I am sure that the garments that they were accustomed to wearing were fine garments. They would not be looked upon as filthy rags, but as desirable clothing. And yet God required them to lie that clothing aside in order to be clothed in the priestly garments. I believe that the Lord may require many of us to give up certain things that seem noble and wonderful in order for Him to use us in the office of the priest.

My wife, Kathleen, and I have already seen this process begin in our lives. There have been several things that we have been asked by the Lord to lay aside so that He could re-clothe us in His purposes and destiny. The stripping process has been very life changing for us. One of the major areas that we saw stripped away had to do with our employment and financial comfort. Both of us were working at great companies and making fairly good money when the Lord asked us to lay those things aside. He then proceeded to shift us into an entirely different direction. It has not always been easy. In fact, at times it has been far from easy. And yet we know that it was a necessary step in the process of becoming carriers of God's glory.

Just as it was with the priests of old, humility is crucial to the next move of God. The Lord will often humble us, and strip us right out in front of others. Aaron and His sons were stripped out in the open, outside the entrance of the tabernacle. Jesus, our High Priest, was also stripped out in the open. Humility is always a requirement for priesthood. As you are stripped of the old mantles and the old garments, don't expect to be able to keep it all hidden from the view of others. The Lord will often make us vulnerable so that He can work humility into our lives.

After the stripping comes the washing. Aaron and his sons were washed from head to toe in water. This is the purification process. Not only does the Lord strip us of the old garments that we use to hold dear, but He then begins to purify us. None of us take a shower fully clothed; because if we did, we would not be able to clean every member of our body. The same is true in the spirit. The Lord must first take us out of the old so that He can truly purify us and put us into the new.

As you are probably already aware, water is a Biblical representation of the Word of God. Aaron and his sons were washed with water; in the same way we must be washed by the Word of the Lord.

As you are reading this book you are probably already feeling the drawing of the Lord to the outer courts. Maybe you have even begun to experience the stripping of your old garments. If you are like me, you do not take pleasure in being stripped and you especially don't enjoy the vulnerable feeling of being naked and exposed. Well I have good news for you. According to this scriptural principle, the fastest way to start the re-clothing process is to get clean. It is time to dig into the Word of God. The Word is the water that brings about the washing and purification process. After adequate washing has taken place, then the Lord will begin to re-clothe you, but not until the washing is complete.

Following the purification process, Moses started to re-dress Aaron and his sons in the new priestly garments. The first garment placed on the priests was the tunic. The tunic was a pure white linen garment that resembled a long night shirt. This garment was to be worn against the skin of the priests underneath their robes.

To us today the pure-white tunic represents righteousness and humility. After we have been stripped and washed then the Lord places on us a garment of His righteousness and humility. His righteousness is to be worn closest to our skin. It is worn underneath the priestly robes. We are to hold the righteousness of God closer to us than the priestly robes.

The priestly robes represent our calling. The righteousness of God must always be of greater importance to us than our calling is. So often we get these two backwards. We put a greater value on our positions, callings and giftings than we do the righteousness of God.

The Bible tells us to seek first the Kingdom of God and His righteousness, and then all the other things will be added to us. The robe of Righteousness always comes first. It has to be what we hold the closest to our heart. We can not properly fulfill our calling until we allow The Lord to clothe us in His righteousness.

Once the Lord clothes us in His righteousness, He then places on us the Robe of Authority. The priestly robe worn by Aaron and his sons were symbols of Authority to the people. As modern day priests we will also be clothed in robes of authority. The Lord will not only give us authority over our enemy, but also governmental and territorial authority in the earth. With the coming outpouring of God's glory there will be an authority that will arise within the body of Christ like we have never seen before. As ambassadors of the Kingdom of Heaven, we will possess the land and speak into the governments of the earth in greater measure than we have in the past. The Lord wants to array His bride with garments of Authority in this hour. However, you can not expect to be clothed in these garments until you are first stripped, washed and re-clothed in His humility and righteousness; only after those three steps are complete can we wear the garments of authority.

Once Moses had clothed the priests with their priestly robes he then gave them their ephods. Ephods are mantles. In scripture, mantles are often used to symbolize anointings and giftings.

In 2 Kings 2 we read about the transferring of Elijah's anointing onto Elisha. The Bible tells us that the mantle of Elijah fell down from the heavens and Elisha picked it up. After Elisha picked up the mantle of Elijah, there was an anointing that came and rested upon Elisha. After you and I are given the garments of righteousness and authority, we are then given mantles that represent the giftings and anointings of the priest. Without the Holy Spirit's anointing and giftings we are unable to minister as priests before the glory of the Lord.

After the mantles came the headgear. First the head was covered with a mitre. A mitre was a turban worn by the Priests. Head cover speaks of respect and submission. To this day the Jewish people wear a head covering if they are planning to minister before the Lord in any way. As modern day priests we too need our spiritual heads covered in submission. Our mindsets, our agendas, our opinions, and our dreams need to come under submission to the work of the Lord.

On top of the mitre, Moses placed on each priest a crown. When I began to study the priestly crown, I learned that the crown was used as a marking. Many Israelites wore turbans, but the priest's turbans were marked by God as someone who was set apart and separated for the work of the Lord. The crown spoke of a Nazarite call placed on the priests; a call of consecration and separation unto the Lord. If you want to be a modern day priest, you must be willing to allow the Lord to mark you, set you apart, and you must be ready to follow higher standards that come with being consecrated unto the Lord.

After the redressing came the blood and the oil anointings. Moses took fresh blood from the sacrifice and placed the blood on the right earlobes, the right thumbs and the right big toes of the priests. Blood symbolizes death. For us it symbolizes the death of Christ on the cross. The placement of the blood on Aaron and his sons was a prophetic picture of what Christ would do in the future. Jesus became our High Priest and yet He also became our sacrifice. He became death for us.

We have all heard the phrase "Dead Man Walking". It is a phrase that is used in the prison system to indicate that a man is taking his last few steps as he walks to the death chamber where his life will end. It is at that moment that the prisoner knows that there is no more life ahead of him. He realizes that it is truly over. No more sunrises, no more sunsets, no more tomorrows. When Jesus carried His cross down the Via Delarosa, He knew that His earthly life was about to end. Some may say that Jesus was a "Dead Man Walking". The major difference, however, between Jesus and those sentenced to die today is that Jesus could still see life ahead of Him. He knew that He was about to end His earthly life in the physical, but he could see past the limitations of his physical life and observe what lie ahead.

You and I are also called to be walking dead men and women. We are to die daily. The Bible says that we are crucified with Christ, so that we no longer live but Jesus lives through us. Furthermore, the Bible tells us to daily pick up our cross. Many of us want to be priests unto the Lord but we do not want to experience the death chamber. As a priest, you and I must be marked with death just like Aaron and his sons, because it is that very mark of death that gives us access to the glory of God. Priests must be marked with the blood or they can not minister before God's glory.

After the first blood anointing came the sprinkling of blood and oil onto the outer garments of the priests. When I first begin to study this anointing ceremony all I could think about was the stains that oil and blood would make on the new clothes. Remember the outer garments were the robe of authority and the ephod of anointing. These were the garments that everyone saw. Here we see that the will of God was to permanently stain these new garments.

Many of us carry around some stains from our past and because of them we often find ourselves thinking that we are in some way disqualified from doing the great works of the Lord. We try to conceal our stains so that no one will see them. Interestingly, here we see that the Lord required the stains to show. He didn't sprinkle blood and oil on the undergarments; He sprinkled them on the outer garments. It was God's plan to permanently stain the visible garments of the priests.

We know that blood represents Christ death and redemption through the cross, and that oil represents the Holy Spirit. We also know that the robes that were stained represent both authority and anointing. As priests, we are given spiritual gifts of authority and gifts of anointing, but those gifts must always be covered by the redemptive message of the cross and directed by the leading of the Holy Spirit.

In the last couple of decades the church has seen several gifted ministers take their giftings for granted and fail to keep themselves submitted to the cross of Christ and the leading of the Holy Spirit. This always brings hurt and division to the body. Even in the Old Testament many of the priests misused their authority and brought shame to the office of the priesthood.

-Humility is the Key-

As modern day priests, we can never take for granted the gifts that God gives us. We must always keep ourselves submitted to the cause of Christ and the leading of the Spirit. I can not state this enough; it is extremely crucial that we stay submitted to God. Humility is the key. If we don't minister out of a heart of humility, we will not be able to flow in the full measure of glory that the Lord longs to release through us into the earth. In fact, pride will stop the flow of God's glory quicker than anything. It was pride that caused Uzzah to misunderstand God's glory. It was pride that caused Eli's son's to misuse God's glory. It was pride that stripped Lucifer from his position in Heaven where he literally dwelled in the glory of God. Pride has always been and will continue to be the number one enemy of God's glory.

After the Blood and the Oil was placed on the priests, they were allowed to enter the tabernacle. The Bible tells us that they remained in the tabernacle for seven days. They were not permitted to leave, nor were they allowed to minister. They were to simply wait.

As priests, we too are often called into a time of waiting. Waiting is one of the most difficult things for us to do, especially today. We are accustomed to having things happen on our time schedule, and when they don't, we often find ourselves irritated and frustrated. It is very important though that we learn to wait on the Lord's timing.

The Lord has a sovereign timing for His glory to be dispersed into the earth. We have already begun to witness the beginning of this great move. Right now, it is very important that we do not presume to understand every direction that God is leading us. Often we will try and go ahead of God, thinking we are "preparing the way of the Lord", when in reality God is about to make a change of direction and we have run out ahead and are unaware of this change.

When I opened this chapter I mentioned the ingredients of a recipe. We must be faithful to prepare the ingredients that God has given us, but we must not attempt to guess what the next ingredients are to be. Submitting to the timing of The Lord is a lesson we must learn now, so that we will be better equipped for this next great move of God's glory.

As we look back over the last few pages we see that The Lord does indeed have a process of preparation for priesthood. I believe that process is still in effect today. First we must go to the outer courts of worship where we allow Him to strip and wash us. Then He will clothe us with His garments of righteousness, authority, and anointings.

We also must be marked with death. We must be willing to die to ourselves and to our agendas daily. We can not afford to allow ourselves to be motivated by selfishness. We must become "Dead men walking" if you will.

It is crucial that we stay submitted to The Holy Spirit and to the cause of Christ. And we must learn to wait on the Lord's timing. Only move when we are told to move. This is the calling of the priests.

Yes, it is a call to death, to purity and to submission, but it is also a call to move in God's authority and giftings. It should not be seen as a drudgery but as a privilege. It is a privilege to be a carrier of God's glory. It is a privilege to walk in the authority and the anointing of the Spirit. We should even see it as a privilege to die to ourselves and allow the Lord to purify us, because the purification process is what gives us access to the anointing.

There is a call to priesthood ringing out in the earth today. I believe that this call has targeted you today. It is beckoning you! You now have a choice. Will you answer the call? Will you allow yourself to be stripped, washed and re-clothed in the righteousness of God? Will you be a conduit of God's glory in the earth? If you will, then The Lord will place upon you His robe of authority and His mantles of anointing. You will have the privilege of carrying the glory of God in the earth, and ministering His glory to this generation.

Chapter Five

Who Do You Think You Are?

Knowing your true Identity in Christ Jesus

Several years ago I worked at a hotel as the desk manager. One afternoon, as I was covering the lunch break for one of my desk clerks, a notably well dressed and obviously financially secure lady came into the lobby inquiring if we had a non-smoking, ground-floor room available. I told her that I was all out of non-smoking rooms, but I could place her in a standard room on the second floor. She was not at all happy with my suggestion. She accused me of lying to her, saying that all the non-smoking rooms could not have been rented already, because there were only a half-dozen cars in the parking lot. I told her that all the non-smoking rooms were reserved by other guests coming in that evening, and they simply had not arrived yet.

She became extremely angry and began to curse and yell. She looked me straight in the eyes and said, "I demand to see the person in charge around here. Who do you think you are, anyway?" I looked back across the desk and smiled as I said, "Well, actually ma'am, I am the person in charge around here." With that she grabbed her purse in a huff and walked out of the hotel.

Have you ever been asked the question, *"Who do you think you are?"* I don't believe that I have ever heard that question used in a positive way. It seems to always be a negative question, and it is usually thrown in your face like some sort of personal attack. Nevertheless, it is a valid question, and I believe that in the context of this book, it is also an extremely important one. Just who do we think we are? Do we truly know who we are? Do we know who we are in Christ? If not, then do we risk the chance of missing out on all that The Lord has for us? Each of us should make it a habit of asking ourselves this question. "Who do I think I am in Christ Jesus?"

As priests it is pertinent that we know the answer. If we do not, then we will have a difficult time embracing the priestly call that God has placed on our lives.

The road ahead of us is guaranteed to stretch us from time to time. There will be moments when it will require us to give up things that we do not want to. If we do not truly know who we are in Christ Jesus, we will not see the true value of laying down our rights and desires in order to become a priest before the Lord. We need our identity firmly secure in Christ.

-You are a Member of Royalty-

A few years ago, *Walt Disney Pictures* produced a movie called *"The Princess Diaries"*. In this movie a royal princess named Amelia was raised as a simple middle class child far away from her country by her mother. Not only did she live far away from the kingdom, but she also never knew who she truly was. Her mother never told her that she was a royal princess. Amelia's mother did not want her to know anything about her former life or the royal lineage that she came from. So, Amelia grew up in San Francisco, California completely oblivious to the lifestyle that she was intended to live.

According to the movie, when Amelia was fifteen years old her father, the reigning Prince of Genovia, died in a terrible accident. Her grandmother, the Queen of Genovia, came to San Francisco to find her. By birthright Amelia was next in line for the throne, but of course Amelia had no idea. As the story unfolds, you watch as she comes to discover that she is in fact a royal princess and that it is her turn to take over the leadership of a nation that she knows nothing about. It is a funny movie about a simple young girl who finds out the hard way who she truly is.

I believe that the church today is a lot like Princess Amelia. We are all members of a royal family and yet we are clueless to what all that means. We are the children of the King of kings and yet we act as if we are only slaves and servants. We have allowed ourselves to become confused by the enemy. Satan does not want us to know our true identity.

I believe the enemy has placed blinders on the church in the hope of keeping us from understanding the truth. It is a simple truth, therefore it should not be difficult to understand and believe, yet sometimes the simplest truths are the ones so easily overlooked. Let's take a look at what the scriptures say about our identity.

In Romans 8:16-17 we read;

"The Spirit Himself bears witness with our spirit that we are children of God, and if children, then heirs – heirs of God and joint heirs with Christ, if indeed we suffer with Him, that we may also be glorified together." (NKJV)

I realize that you have already heard this before. You know that you are God's child, but have you ever really allowed the fullness of what that means to sink in? Have you ever taken the time to really ponder the awesomeness of being an heir of Father God?

-Freedom in the House-

When you were a child growing up in your parent's house, did you have to ring the doorbell in order to enter your own home? Of course not! You were a member of the family. You could walk right in. Neither did you have to ask for permission to get a drink of water. You had access to the glasses and to the kitchen sink anytime you wanted. As you got a little older you could even help yourself to the juice in the refrigerator, or to the food in the cupboard. There was freedom in the house for the members of the household to utilize what the house had to offer.

You were also free to enter the various rooms in your parent's home. You could relax in the living room, or take a shower in the bathroom, or kick back and read a book on the rear deck, all without having to ask permission. If you needed something, then you just went and got it. It wasn't only your parent's home; it was your home too.

So if we are called the children of the Father, then it is correct to say that we are family members in Father's house. As family members we have full access to the Lord's house and everything that is in it. We can go to the refrigerator when we are hungry. We can get a drink when we are thirsty. We can rest when we are weary. The Lord wants us to make ourselves at home in His house.

This may seem like a simplistic truth, but oddly enough many Christians either consciously or subconsciously believe that they have no access to the things of God. They do not see themselves as worthy enough to go after and take a hold of the many blessings that

God has to offer His children. Many of us have been Christians for a long time and therefore have been members of Father's house for many years; yet we have never taken the time to look around. Many of us still do not know what is behind those big doors inside of Father's house.

-A Tour of Father's House-

Father's House is an enormous house! It is full of treasures and riches for us to enjoy. Like any home, there are some things that the children have access to all the time (i.e. a drink from the kitchen, a snack from the fridge, the bathroom, the couch, their bedrooms, the dining table etc.). Then there are things that children must have permission to use (such as the stove, the knives, the antiques, the power tools in the garage, the Back yard BBQ, etc.). These things require maturity. Parents only allow their children access to these things when they know the child is responsible enough to use them appropriately.

Let's take a look at these different categories. Let's take a tour around the house of our Father and see what is waiting there for us to discover.

First there are things in Father's house that we all have access to all the time. I believe that these are the things we need on a regular basis. These are also the most important things to our Christian walk. Things like forgiveness; contentment; peace; love; joy; the power of God; truth; wisdom; health; provisions; and the list goes on and on.

We have access to these things all the time. We do not need prior authorization to utilize them; we can simply go and get them. They are available to us 24 hours a day. If you look at the above list and you say, "I don't have some of those things operating in my life", then you need to know that they are accessible for the taking. If you do not have peace, then go after it. It is available for you right now. If you do not have joy, then the Lord wants you to go and get your fill. Father's house is stocked with an ample supply of blessings and provisions that we can go and partake of whenever we want and as much as we need.

The problem is we do not realize that these things are constantly available to us. We see ourselves as visitors in Father's house. We act like orphans in the very house that we belong to. The enemy has placed an orphan spirit over the body of Christ. Because of this orphan spirit, we often view ourselves as too unworthy to really be comfortable in Father's house. I believe we insult the Father's heart when we act like guests in our own home.

Could you imagine if you had to get your kids a glass of water every time they needed one, just because they were uncomfortable getting one themselves? It is understandable when your guests act that way but not your kids. Not only would it get old real fast, but you would also begin to wonder what is making your children feel so uncomfortable. Father wants us to feel at home in His house.

-Spiritual Maturity from God's Perspective-

There are some things in Father's house, however, that we must have His permission to use. With these come certain levels of accountability. These are things like financial riches; particular prophetic giftings; the secrets of His kingdom; gifts of healing; power to raise the dead; the ability to perform the miraculous; etc.

These things require a level of spiritual responsibility before the Lord will allow us to utilize them. Please do not misunderstand me here; I am not talking about seasoned sainthood. The Lord releases miraculous gifts upon baby Christians all the time. It is not a question of age or how long you have been saved; it is a question of responsibility. Can the Lord trust you to utilize these gifts for His divine will and purposes, or will you use them to further your own agenda?

Too often, if we are not careful, we will prejudge someone's spiritual giftings based solely on the fact that they are still young believers. How often have you heard someone say, "Don't put to much stock in what he has to say because he is still *young in the Lord*." Although this is true some of the time, we must not make it a habit of prejudging someone's spiritual abilities based solely on how long they have been saved. Since God can see past someone's outer shell and focus on the intentions of their heart, He knows when they are ready to move into more advanced spiritual giftings.

I am a woodworker with a work shop in my garage and there are 12 year olds who I would have not problem lending one of my power saws to because they have been properly trained to use it. At the same time, there are 25 year olds that I probably would not trust with the power saw simply because they have never used one before. It is not a question of age; it is a question of understanding and responsibility. This same principle can be applied to the advanced things of the Spirit. The Lord wants to train us to use them correctly and responsibly.

In the same way that we would not give a rifle to a 9 year old, the Lord may withhold certain giftings and anointings until particular times in our lives. I believe that The Father wants every one of His children to mature to the place where they can be allowed to use all the things in Father's house. As the body of Christ, The Bible calls us the hands and the feet of God to the earth. I believe that The Father longs to release authoritative, miraculous signs and wonders into the earth, and we are the venue that He has chosen to use. As God's children, we must be trustworthy to carry these things out into the earth for the purpose of furthering the Kingdom of God.

Back to our original question! *Who do you think you are?* According to God's Word you are a child of God with full access to all that He has. You are a member of the royal family of God. You can feel free to roam around the house of Your Heavenly Father and make yourself at home. You can go and get the things you need. And as a trustworthy, submitted child of God, you have access to the authoritative, miraculous gifts of the Spirit.

-You are Part of a Royal Priesthood-

But who else are you? Not only are you a child of The Father, but you are also a priest of His glory. Revelations 1:6 says that we are both Kings and Priests before the Lord. In Revelations 5 it continues to say that we shall reign on the earth with the Lord as Kings and Priests.

In 1 Peter 2:9 it says;

But you are a chosen people, a royal priesthood, a holy nation, a people belonging to God, that you may declare the praises of Him who called you out of darkness and into His wonderful light. (NIV)

We have all been called to the office of priesthood. You don't have to take my word for it; the Lord has already said it in His Word. As priests, we not only have personal access to the glory of God, but we have been chosen by the Lord to carry His glory out into the earth. As we have already studied in an earlier chapter there is a call going out for a generation of priests to rise up and usher in this new realm of God's glory in the earth. This is not a call to a specific, small amount of people; this is a call to everyone. It is not a question of calling; it is a question of choosing. As priests who know their true identity in Christ, we must choose to answer this call.

-*You are a Child of Covenant*-

There is yet another important aspect of our identity that the enemy tries to keep us from discovering. The enemy does not want us to fully understand that we are also the children of Abraham. Satan would want you to believe that if you are not Jewish then you are not a child of Abraham. But according to Romans 11:17 we have been grafted into Abraham's family tree.

Maybe you are asking yourself the question, "Why is it so important that I know that I am grafted into Abraham's tree?" It is important because it makes you a Child of Covenant. The Lord has made some huge promises to the Children of Abraham, and you have not only been grafted into the Abrahamic family line, but you have also been grafted into the Abrahamic Covenant. Many times when we read the scriptures, we do not claim all the promises written therein. The reason is because we see those promises as for Israel only and not for us. But according to Romans 11:17 they are for us as well.

When you graft a branch into a tree the branch becomes part of that tree. It gets its nourishment from the roots of that tree just like all the other branches. The tree does not play favorites with its branches, it simply distributes the nutrients coming up from the roots and each branch is supplied for.

When we accepted Christ as savior, we were grafted into the tree of Abraham. Therefore we are now a part of the covenantal people of God. The promises in the Word regarding the seed of Abraham are our promises as well.

-Getting to Know Your New Root System-

The mistake so many believers make today is they do not know their new root system. They can't get past the graft. They see the graft as a point of separation. The graft was never intended to act as a dividing line between the natural and the grafted branches. Instead it was intended to be a place where Jews and Gentiles were all joined together. The blood of Jesus is the graft that connects us to God's chosen people. Not only are we connected to God's chosen people through the blood but we actually become a part of God's chosen people through the blood of Christ. Jesus is the Vine and we are His branches firmly grafted in.

Regardless of what trees we used to belong to, we now belong to the covenantal tree of Abraham. The nutrients that we now rely on to sustain us are coming from the roots of our new tree not our old one. We must get past the graft and learn who we are in Christ.

When we know who we are, then we can walk in the authority of who we are. If you are hired to be the CEO of your company, then you know that you can walk in the authority of your office. When you discover who you are in Christ, then you will begin to fully operate in the authority of your office as a member of the body of Christ.

-Proper Identification-

You may be asking yourself, what does this chapter have to do with the glory of God? The answer is a simple one; without a healthy identity in Christ, you will have a difficult time being a carrier of God's glory.

First of all, those who doubt their God given identity often doubt their worth. And those who doubt their worth almost always doubt their call. As sinful men and women, it is true that we are unworthy of any good thing that The Lord has to give, but when we discover our new identity as priests of His glory, the covenantal children of Abraham, and as sons and daughters of Father God, then we are able to move past feelings of inadequacy and unworthiness and into an understanding of son-ship.

Secondly, those who doubt their God given identity often doubt their ability. The Lord wants to equip us to do His will in the earth, but if we are unsure of our identity in Christ then we can easily find ourselves doubting our ability to accomplish His will. Knowing who you are helps you realize what you can accomplish.

As those called to be priests before the glory of God we must have a firm understanding of who we are. Powerful, authoritative, and miraculous gifts of The Spirit will accompany His glory. We must come to realize that as His children we have an inherent authority that allows us to operate in these gifts. However we must prove ourselves trustworthy to carry out only the will and desires of Heaven.

So let me ask you again, just who do you think you are? Your answer must not come simply from your understanding; it must come from your heart. It is not enough to simply know the right answer; you have to believe it. So, who are you? What are you capable of accomplishing for the Kingdom of God? Do you believe that you truly can do as Philippians 4:13 says? Do you believe that you really can do '*all things*' through Christ's who gives you strength? Many Christians would have to answer no to that last question. Many of us find it difficult to truly believe in our ability to do the things that The Lord has called us to do. Ah, but there is an answer to this dilemma. The answer lies in our identity. Once our identity is firmly founded in the Lord and His promises, than I believe we can boldly answer that last question with a definite YES.

Chapter Six

The Greatest Call of the Priests

To Love Him and Worship Him with Everything we Possess

When I was in Bible College, I remember sitting around with a group of students and discussing what each of us thought our individual 'callings' were. Some said they were called to pastor, others said they were called to foreign missions. The rambunctious ones believed they were called to be youth evangelists and the talented ones declared they were called to the make a fortune in the Christian music industry. Each one of us wore our "callings" proudly like a merit badge or a gold metal. It seemed so important in those days to know exactly what God was calling you to be. In fact if you were not certain of your exact calling, then you were just not as spiritual as the rest of us. Your calling became part of your identity.

Over the years I have kept in contact with several of those students, and believe it or not, very few of them actually ended up doing what they thought they were called to do. Some of those who thought they were called to pastor are now missionaries, and some that thought they were going into the music industry are now pastoring. In fact many individuals who saw themselves as full time church employed ministers have actually became business men and women and are ministering in the marketplace. In college I thought I was called to be a traveling evangelist, and it turned out that after college I spent the next 15 years as a worship leader.

It is easy to become consumed with trying to figure out God's will for your life. God's will is not always an exact calling or job description. The truth is The Lord usually reveals His plan for your life in segments over the years. My Father used to say that you don't need to know every stretch of the highway in order to drive on it; you just need to pay attention to the stretch that you are driving down right now. The same is true with the leading of the Lord; you don't have to have the whole picture in order to stay in God's perfect will.

-Your Highest Calling-

There is a high calling, however, that you can be certain of. It is the greatest call that you will ever have.

It is a call to every believer and we are all called to this together. You don't have to go to seminary to discover what it is, and it is not based on your abilities or spiritual gifting. The highest call of every believer is also the greatest commandment in the Bible. Our greatest call is to be intimately and passionately in love with our God.

It is recorded in the book of Mark that the religious leaders of the day came to Jesus and asked Him a rather peculiar question. Their motive, of course, was to trick Christ so that they could discredit Him. They asked Him, "Teacher, of all the commandments, which one is the greatest commandment?" The answer that Jesus gave them is recorded in Mark 12:30.

Mark 12:30 says:

"And thou shalt love the Lord thy God with all thy heart, and with all thy soul, and with all thy mind, and with all thy strength: This is the first commandment." (KJV)

According to Jesus, the greatest commandment we have is to love the Lord. But not simply love him like you would every other person on the planet. Mark 12 is not talking about a casual form of love. This is not the kind of love you would have with a close friend or family member. In fact, this is even greater that the love found between husbands and wives. The love spoken of in Mark 12:30 should surpass any other passion that you and I have ever expressed, because the Bible tells us that this love requires every part of us. We are to love the Lord with <u>ALL</u> our hearts, <u>ALL</u> our souls, <u>ALL</u> our minds, and <u>ALL</u> our strengths.

Regardless of your "calling", whether you are a missionary, a pastor, a musician, or a bus driver, the utmost calling you have is to adore the Lord. Being the lover of God must be the primary focus of every believer. This is why Jesus called this the *"greatest commandment"* given to us by The Lord. God wants to be intimate with His people. It is not enough for Him to be fervently in love with us, He wants us to also be passionately in love with Him as well.

Throughout the Bible, God used several different relational types to depict our relationship with Him. Some passages in scripture call us the "Servants of God"; other verses say that we are the "Sons of God" or the "Children of God". In the beginning of the Bible we are referred to as the "Handiwork of God, His most precious creation", and then at the close of the Bible, in Revelation we are called "His Glorious Bride". Is it possible to be all these things at the same time? Yes, because we have a multi-faceted relationship with Him. However, over all these relational types, our greatest call is to be the "Lovers of God."

-Lovers of God-

Most Christians can accept being God's servants. They can embrace the fact that they are bond-slaves of the Father. Believers today don't usually have a problem accepting the fact that they are God's children; heirs of the Father and joint-heirs with Christ Jesus. But when you start to talk to Christians about being the intimate bride of Christ, many will start to squirm. Many Believers get a little embarrassed when you speak of being intimate or passionate with The Lord. Why is this? I believe it is because they do not fully understand their highest calling.

It is not possible to love someone with ALL your heart, mind, soul and strength and not have an intimate relationship with them. Intimacy with Him is not a new idea that just started circulating the country these last few years. Intimacy with God was His idea. He is the initiator of this elevated calling.

As we all know, one known by-product of intimacy is pregnancy. Intimacy produces life. The Lord wants to impregnate His people with divine purposes. He wants us to give birth to new and exciting things of the Spirit. How are these new things implanted into us so that we can give birth to them in our lives? They come from being passionately in love with The Lord. They come from spending intimate time with the Lord on a regular basis. One of the best ways to become intimate with The Lord is through worship.

The correct motivation behind our worship should be our passionate love for the Lord. Throughout church history, man has tried to demonstrate their love for God through good works and through keeping the law.

Basically, we think that by simply behaving ourselves, staying obedient, and being good little Christians, The Lord will somehow "get it" that we love Him. Today's church is guilty of believing that it is not necessary to be passionately in love with God. We say things like, "There is just no need to go and get all mushy with the Lord, now is there?" If I was to try that with my wife, I would find out real fast that good behavior is not enough to prove to her that I love her. If I left out all the "mushy stuff", I would quickly discover how imperative that "mushy stuff" truly is to our relationship.

Obedience is important but it is possible to obey someone without loving them. The Bible tells us that we are not saved by our good works, but through faith in Christ. Although it is wonderful to serve the Lord with our good deeds it does not draw us to God, neither does it prove our love for Him.

-Worship is the Key-

So how do we show the Lord we love Him? Once again, the best way is through our worship. If the greatest call of the believer is to be a lover of God, and if worship is one of the best avenues we have to communicate our love for God, then I believe it is safe to also say that the greatest call of every believer is to be an intimate worshiper of God. As lovers of God we are not only to love the Lord with ALL of our heart, mind, soul, and strength, but we should worship Him with ALL of them as well.

The Priests who stood around David's tabernacle day and night had one job to do - continuously worship the Lord with all their hearts, minds, souls, and strength. They were to sing, dance, play their instruments, worship, honor, and glorify the Lord day and night without stopping. Their worship was twenty four hours a day, seven days a week, and three-hundred and sixty-five days a year.

We have already established that The Lord is restoring David's tabernacle in our day. Just as worship continuously and constantly surrounded the tabernacle in David's day; so worship will increase and become a mighty ingredient in the revival of God's glory that He will restore to our generation. Worship is the key!

We are entering into a time where worship must take a front burner position in our lives. It can no longer be a recreational activity that we participate in a few times a week at church; it must become a lifestyle. The restoration of David's Tabernacle is not only a restoration of God's manifest Glory, but it is also a restoration of true worship in the hearts of believers. In order to truly understand how to worship with <u>All</u> our hearts, souls, minds, and strengths we need to understand what these four areas represent.

-All Your Heart-

The word "heart" in the New Testament usually represents the seat of divine influence. The heart was considered to be the center of man's inner life. It is the home of the soul. The heart is where we find man's true character. We personify all kinds of appearances on the outside but the heart is where you find the real deal; the real person. The heart is also the seat of our deepest desires and confidences.

In Mark 12 we are told to love the Lord with *all* of our heart. Notice that the Bible didn't say *from* our heart, but it said *all* our heart. We can not afford to hold back any part of our heart from the Lord. He is asking for it all. What this scripture is telling us is that we are to love Him more than we love any other desire. To love the Lord with all of our heart means to love Him above anything else in our lives. The heart of man is where the throne of man is. As we all know, The Lord is the one who should be sitting on the thrones of our hearts ruling over every area of our lives.

Another verse that comes to mind is Jeremiah 29:13. This verse says that we will find the Lord when we seek for Him with all our hearts. Once again the Lord is saying that when you truly love Him with all your heart, you will find Him. If we want to know the heart of The Father, and be a man or woman "after God's own heart", like David was, then we need to love Him with not *part* but *all* of our hearts.

-All Your Soul-

The next word we see in Mark 12:30 is "soul". Your emotions, desires, wants, likes, dislikes, moods and attitudes all woven together make up your soul. Your soul tells us who you are. Even your personality comes from the soulish part of you. So what this passage in Mark is saying is that you should love the Lord with all of your emotions, all your wants, all your likes, all your moods, and all your attitudes. Even your personality should show your love for God.

Let me put a controversy to rest right here. Your emotion is part of your soul. So if you are to love the Lord with ALL your soul then getting a little emotional sometimes during worship is perfectly Biblical. Many believers today have been told that they must detach themselves from their emotions during times of praise and worship. But frankly, it is impossible to truly worship the Lord with ALL of your soul if you withhold your emotions.

It is true that there are the occasional times of corporate worship where our emotions must be reeled in a bit because of the direction that The Lord is taking the meeting, but most of the time this should not come into play. Furthermore, individually, during your time of personal worship before The Lord, you should never feel that you are not allowed to express yourself emotionally to the Lord. According to Mark 12, God desires all your soul to be connected to Him. That includes your emotions.

-All You Mind-

Mark 12:30 then goes on to say that we are to love the Lord with "all our mind". The mind is where we find our intellect, our knowledge, our wisdom and our thought life. The very things we are thinking should be an expression of our love for the Lord. The things that we entertain in our minds should not only be pleasing to God, but they should also bring Him worship.

Our minds are probably the most difficult area to surrender to the Lord. During times of intimacy with God, there always seems to be a distraction that tries to get our attention and take our focus off of worshiping our God. The mind is the largest spiritual battlefield there is. The enemy knows this battlefield very well. The human mind is very impressionable, and the enemy knows what exactly to throw at each of us. He knows where we are weak.

Our minds may make a good battlefield for the enemy, but it is the passions of our heart and soul that really have the ability to captivate us. Therefore, the best way to overthrow the enemy in the area of your mind is to increase your passion. If you are extremely passionate for the Lord and for His worship, then the enemy will find it very difficult to distract you in the arena of your mind. Also, when we fill our thoughts with the things of God, we can push the enemy back off the battlefield of our minds.

-All Your Strength-

The last word given to us in this passage in Mark 12 is "strength". The Greek word for strength in this passage literally means abilities. The Lord wants us to love Him with all of our abilities. This passage is not speaking only of our physical strength, but our abilities in the areas of gifting and talent as well.

I am reminded of the parable of the talents. In this parable, the third servant after receiving one talent went and hid it in the sand. He was fearful that if he misused it the master would be angry. Hearing the parable, it is easy for us to judge the third servant, but in actuality most of us are guilty of the same thing. The Lord has given to every person gifts and talents, but all too often we allow our talents to lie dormant. We are not always good stewards with the talents that The Lord has given us. Too many of our talents are underdeveloped and inactive. The Lord desires for us to use all our talents, gifts, strengths, and abilities as forms of worship.

In Malachi 1:6-14 God speaks to the nation of Israel regarding their gifts of worship that they are offering in the temple. The children of Israel owned acceptable male lambs and vowed to bring them to the temple to present as a worship sacrifice to the Lord. But then on the day of the sacrifice they left their acceptable, valuable lambs at home and brought the blemished, blind and lame lambs for the sacrifice. Basically they were promising and vowing their finest but then bringing their worst.

God went so far as to say that He would rather someone shut the temple doors than to continue to receive these half-hearted gifts of worship. The Lord said that the children of Israel were actually lighting useless fires on His altar. He was tired of deceitful man giving less than his best.

As worshipers we can learn a lot from Malachi 1. So often we give the Lord less than our best in worship, and yet we expect Him to show up and move in all His glory and power. We think we can please Him with our half-hearted gifts of praise.

-Priests are Called to Give Their All-

Will The Lord say the same thing to us some day that He said to Israel in the days of Malachi? Will He one day shout from Heaven, "Someone please shut the doors of the church and lock them up."? Will He become sick and tired of people not bringing their best? One thing is certain; we know that Father's heart is longing for our best. Mark 12 says that we are to love the Lord with ALL that we are. He wants all our hearts, all our souls, all our minds, and all our strengths. He wants the best we have to offer.

God is looking for priests who will stand and minister in the holy place before His glory. He is searching for worshipers who will take Mark 12 to heart. The Lord has a particular passion for those whose greatest desire is to love and worship Him with everything they have.

The Lord is looking for people who will recklessly abandon themselves and give all that they are to their God. When He finds them, He will crown them with His Glory. His highest calling is for you and me to become intimate lovers of God. His desire is that we become so passionately in love with Him that we aggressively worship Him with all of our hearts, souls, minds, and strengths. That kind of worship will usher in the glory of God.

Chapter Seven

The Kabod and the Shekinah

Two Types of Glory Woven Together

When we study the tabernacles of the Old Testament we see that God's glory visited them in more than one way. We have already spoken of the flame of glory that rested between the cherubim on the mercy seat, but there was a second display of God's glory. The Lord also visited the tabernacle through a cloud that settled down upon it. The Hebrew word for the flame on the Ark is "Shekinah". When you study the meaning of this word you find that it means "the *visible sign* of God's presence upon the Ark of the Covenant." The Hebrew word for the cloud that rested upon the tabernacle is "Kabod". The meaning of this word is "the *weighty presence* and honor of God." I want to take a moment and look at these two types of glory. I believe that they will give us keys to understanding what we are about to see and experience in the coming move of God.

In the book of Exodus, chapters 25-40 we find the historical account of the building of Moses' tabernacle. In these scriptures, Moses is given the schematics for each piece of furniture that is to be used in the tabernacle, as well as the blueprints for the tabernacle itself. In chapter 40, verses 33-34, we read that after everything was built and put in place, then the glory came. Exodus tells us that a cloud (the Kabod) covered the tent of meeting and when it did, the glory of God filled the tabernacle. Moses was not able to go inside because the Kabod of God was too heavy.

As we study the tabernacle we see that the Kabod never truly left. The cloud simply lifted off the tabernacle and rested in the sky directly above it. When night fell, the cloud would be replaced by a pillar of fire; then in the morning the cloud would return and the fire would leave.

-The Deposit and The Depositor-

So when did the Shekinah flame of God first appear between the cherubim? It showed up when the Kabod showed up. When the Kabod of God filled the tabernacle it left a deposit in the house. That deposit was the Shekinah.

Why is this so important to us today? Does it really matter to you and to me that the Kabod brought a deposit of the Shekinah? Yes it does! The reason it does is because we need the Shekinah of God. The Shekinah carries a noticeable, visible aspect that we must have for the end time harvest. We need the identifiable glory of God in our local fellowships and in our homes.

Remember in David's tabernacle, it was the Shekinah of God that was visible to both the Jews and the Gentiles. It is the Shekinah that The Lord wants to restore to our generation. So how does it come? It comes with the Kabod. The Kabod brings the Shekinah. Therefore, in order to receive the Shekinah glory of God we first must embrace the Kabod of God.

-Embracing the Kabod-

What is the Kabod of God? As we have already stated, the Kabod is the *weighty presence* and honor of God. You have probably already experienced the Kabod of God multiple times in your life. There are times during corporate worship, when God's presence literally feels thick and heavy in the service. This overwhelming sense of God's weighty presence is a small portion of His Kabod. When you sense this taking place, you are experiencing one of the initial aspects of His glory.

During the Brownsville Revival and the Toronto Outpourings many people said they felt as if they were being pinned to the floor by some heavy object. Many others said that they felt as if someone very large was sitting on them. Other times entire corporate bodies have felt as if the weighty presence of The Lord was hovering in the building. I believe that what these people were experiencing was the Kabod of God.

In the last decade of Renewal, we have seen the Lord manifest His presence in this way countless times. What is The Lord trying to do when His presence is sitting on you or pinning you to the floor? He is longing to deposit His Shekinah inside you. He wants to pour out His glory upon His people.

-Waves of Kabod and Showers of Shekinah-

In August, 2002, the Lord gave me a prophetic vision of His Kabod. In the vision I was laying on the floor in my living room praying for God's glory to be poured out on the body of Christ. As I was praying, a wave of the Kabod of God filled the room. I could feel His heavy, weighty presence filling up the place. As I laid there surrounded by the Lords Presence, I began to notice what felt like rain falling inside the room.

At first the rain was like a light shower. I was lying on my face on the floor and I could feel the rain bouncing off my back. As I turned my head to see the rain, I realized that it was not rain I was feeling and hearing, instead I saw tiny gemstones falling around the room. They were so small in size that they sounded and felt like a light sprinkling of rain.

Then the next wave of Kabod came in, and The Lord's presence became heavier than before. As it did, the rain picked up. No longer was it similar to a light shower, but now it resembled a torrential rainstorm. The gemstones had grown in size as well; probably about the size of a one karat diamond. As I looked more closely at the gemstones I could make out what appeared to be diamonds, emeralds, rubies, sapphires, and even pearls. I lay there mesmerized by the beauty of these gleaming stones. Beautiful colors danced before my eyes. Some of these stones where gems that I had never seen before in the natural and so I was unable to determine what kind of stones they were.

Then, as if a third wave crashed over me, I felt the Kabod of God grow even heavier. Again the rain picked up. Now it was like a hail storm. The gemstones were very large now, some measuring over one inch in diameter. This sounds like an awesome wonderful experience, but in reality it was a bit frightening. When this third wave of Kabod fell, there was an intense realization of God's holiness and infinite power that accompanied His Kabod. The stones were no longer my primary focus; the holiness of God was. As awesome as these huge gemstones were they could no longer hold my attention. All I could think about was God's holiness and my lack of holiness.

I found myself in the middle of an inward battle. I wanted so much to experience His manifest presence and yet I wanted to get up and run away from His awesome holiness. If I could have dug a hole in the carpet and crawled through the floor I would have. Not because the experience was bad, it was actually very wonderful, yet there was a holy fear that was present at the same time. It is difficult for me to communicate this experience with words that actually do it justice. I knew that I was unworthy of such a visitation, and I found myself becoming fearful. I realized just how frail and weak I was and how great and mighty God's glory was. I could not help but wonder how a mere man could be a carrier of God's glory. I knew that I was still only experiencing a small portion of the Lord's Kabod and yet I knew that it had the power to actually destroy me.

By this time the Kabod was so heavy in my vision that I asked the Lord to please stop. I felt as if I would not be able to breath. After a few moments the Kabod lifted a little, then a little more, and soon I was able to stand. The presence of the Lord remained thick all over the room but the rain had stopped and the weighty Kabod had subsided enough for me to stand up.

As my vision continued, I got up and looked around the room. Everywhere I looked I saw sparkling gemstones. They were well over a foot deep on the living room floor. They were also piled up on every level surface, as well as on all the furniture, the plants, the television, the stereo. It was a beautiful glorious mess.

Next, I tried to make sense of the gemstones. I began to gather them up according to their colors and size. I tried to separate them by placing them in large 33 gallon plastic bags according to their color. To my surprise the gemstones were so heavy that the bags began to rip. Besides, there were just too many of them to separate. As I gave up on trying to organize and separate them, I had an overwhelming sense that I was not supposed to organize them. This was a God move; and man and all his wisdom was not to attempt to control or organize this mighty move of God.

When the vision was over, I began to seek the Lord for the meaning of the gemstones I had seen. The Lord told me that His Kabod will visit His people in a powerful way, and that it will come with a deposit of His supernatural Shekinah, just as it did in Moses' tabernacle. If you are like me, you really want the Shekinah of God to come and be manifested in your life and you can't wait to get to the supernatural stuff. But all too often we try and skip step one in a hurry to reach step two. We must first embrace the Kabod of God if we are to receive the impartation of His Shekinah. We must first embrace His presence and His Honor. We must first seek Him and then we will be in the proper position to receive His outpouring.

As the Lord continued to speak to me, He explained that the gemstones in the vision represented the Shekinah deposit that the Lord longs to bring to His people. As I listened to the Lord, He told me that the gemstones in my vision represent the numerous miracles that will take place in our day. Some of them will seem small and others will seem large but each of them will be an undeniable miracle, and The Lord would receive all the glory for them.

The Lord began to show me the types of miracles that will accompany an outpouring of His glory. He showed me creative miracles of healing as well as instantaneous miracles of deliverance. He showed me miracles of provision and finance. As I continued to commune with the Lord, He also showed me some more uncommon and unconventional miracles that the Lord wants to restore to the body of Christ such as the ability to speak to the natural elements of the earth and they obey us, or the ability to be transported from one place to another, or the ability to perform signs and wonders. These miracles happened in the Bible and were for the purposes of bringing glory to God and authenticity to His love and power.

The Lord reminded me of Peter; how his shadow healed the sick and the afflicted as he walked pass them. He also reminded me that Peter was in the upper room when the Kabod of God moved in like a mighty rushing wind and deposited the Shekinah flame of God on the heads of the saints there. I heard the Lord Say, "just as it was in Moses' tabernacle, and just as it was in the upper room on the day of Pentecost, so it will be in your generation".

-A Sign to the Unbeliever-

He then reminded me that the very definition of the word Shekinah is that it is "a visible sign". He also reminded me that the purpose of the miraculous is for it to be a "sign" to the unbeliever. The Lord told me that He is visiting His people with His Kabod so that He can once again deposit His Shekinah so that His Shekinah can draw the lost and the broken to cross of Christ.

The Kabod and the Shekinah are joined at the hip. They are different forms of God's glory but they are woven together. One is the *depositor* and the other one is the *deposit*. You can't have the Shekinah without the Kabod. In our day we must embrace both the Kabod and the Shekinah of God.

Many times we can get confused when we study the glory of God. Some say that the Lord's glory falls from heaven, rises upon the land and fills corporate groups and meetings. This is why we have so many songs in regards to God's glory falling on us. Others disagree and say that the glory is deposited inside of us by the Holy Spirit and flows out of us individually. The fact is both are true. The Kabod of God does fall from heaven during times of corporate worship and it is the Shekinah that the Lord wants to deposits within each of us.

In the upper room on the day of Pentecost, It was the Holy Spirit who brought the Kabod and the Shekinah. The Kabod accompanied the Holy Spirit and the deposit of Shekinah that followed were cloven tongues of fire upon the heads of the believers. Also, many spiritual gifts were deposited into each believer and from there they carried the glory of God out into the earth.

In 2 Corinthians 3:18 we read that we are being "changed from glory to glory by the Spirit of the Lord". I believe that each of us is given new levels of God's glory at different stages of our lives. When we were filled with the Holy Spirit, we experienced a Kabod move of God that left a deposit of the Lord's Shekinah in the form of Spiritual gifts (Tongues, prophecy, faith etc.), but just as we read in 2 Corinthians 3:18 we are being changed from glory to glory. The Lord wants to continue to deposit new levels of His Shekinah within us.

I believe that the church is about to go up another level. We are entering into a time of transition where we will experience another change "from glory to glory" just like the Bible said we would. We are living in the day that Amos spoke of. We will see the restoration of David's tent in our generation. We will see the glory of God released again upon the earth. Yesterday's revivals were great for yesterday, but they fail to compare to the glory that is ahead of us. It is time we fix our eyes on what is ahead instead of what is behind.

-Changing Your Perspective-

For too long we have looked back at our history when we wanted to see great moves of God. What causes people to look back? One reason we look back is because we believe that the past moves of God were greater than what we are presently experiencing. I believe the days of looking back are over. The move of God that has begun will be greater than any other in the history of the church.

Over the past several years I have heard minister after minister speak with great fondness to the move of God in the 60's and 70's. They usually are referring to the "Jesus Movement" or the "Catholic Renewal". And as you listen to them you can still hear their hearts longing for the good old days.

More recently, I have heard Christians tell of the wonderful things that took place in the mid 90's when renewal came to their church. They are constantly trying to figure out why renewal stopped. Who killed it? What did we do wrong? I personally do not believe that renewal has stopped. I believe that the Lord is simply positioning us to move into the next wave of His glory. Many people, however, are stuck looking back at the past and are unable to see what is coming.

The main reason people look back with fondness to the so called "glory days" is because they have no vision for what is ahead. They are so busy re-living the past that they haven't asked the Lord for a vision of the future. The Bible tells us that without a vision the people perish. We need to notice and identify that the true "glory days" are just ahead of us.

The past moves of God were wonderful. They are a testimony of the faithfulness of Our Heavenly Father. But what is the purpose of a testimony? It is to cause us to rise up as men and women of faith and believe that The Father will do the same again in our day. Testimonies are not to keep us looking back but to encourage us to embrace the revelation of what lies ahead. We need to catch the vision of what The Lord is about to do in our day.

Unfortunately, we are not the first generation of "look backers". The children of Israel looked back as they made their way across the desert for their promised land. On many occasions they found themselves believing that they would rather return to old familiar Egyptian slavery, than to make their way to a promised land that they had never seen. Why were they constantly looking back? Because even though they had heard the prophetic Word of the Lord and even though they knew God had made a covenant with them to take them to their own land, they still never fully got it. They never truly embraced the vision of what lay ahead of them.

Because of this, when they actually reached their destination, they still would not receive the words of Joshua and Caleb. Even when they stood at the very doorstep to the promises they had been given, they still would not believe. They allowed their present opposition to keep them from embracing their destiny as a nation.

Another Biblical example of a "look backer" is Lot's wife. Genesis 19 tells the story of Lot fleeing Sodom and Gomorra with his wife and two daughters. The Lord told Lot that He would take him to a place of protection in the mountains. The Bible tells us that actual angels came and led them out of the city and away from the danger that was about to be unleashed on the land.

Verse 26 tells us that Lot's wife looked back and God turned her into a pillar of salt. She looked back because she could not see the value of what lay ahead of her. Instead, she longed for what she was leaving behind. The question that demands an answer is how you could still look back after an angelic visitation. It wasn't Lot who warned her that the city was going to be destroyed; it was genuine, bona fide, authentic angelic warriors from heaven that gave her the news. Not only that, but these angelic warriors actually led her out of the city; yet she still looked back.

Our pasts are a powerful thing. They impact our lives with such force that they can easily keep us tied to what we once were, and in doing so, they actually hold us captive from what we can become. We must see the value of what is ahead of us. We must believe the promises of God. It is time to set our faces as flint toward what The Lord is about to do in our midst. We need a paradigm shift. We need our spirits to recognize that the present and the future hold greater things for us than the past did.

Our new paradigms need to be ones that say, "Today is the day for the supernatural power of God to be displayed in our communities and in our churches". For years the Body of Christ has heard prophetic words of a new day that is coming when The Lord's power would be unleashed on the earth. God has promised us over and over that the day is coming when the saints of God would operate in miraculous gifts of healing and deliverance. But our incorrect paradigms have constantly pushed the fulfillment of those prophetic words out into the distant future. But it is time for a paradigm shift. Now is the time, and we are the people!

-The Least of These-

It is already happening in third world countries around the world. Missionaries and Evangelists are seeing great outpourings of God's manifested power. I use to struggle with this and wonder why The Lord has chosen to demonstrate His power in the poor regions of the world first. As I have prayed into this I have come to see a pattern in scripture and in Church history as well. Throughout history we can clearly see that The Lord loves to start great things with the "least of these". He loves to take a timid and shy Gideon and turn him into an Army General. He loves to take simple fishermen and turn them into the world's first evangelists. He loves to take an insignificant barn on Azusa Street in Los Angeles and turn it into a world changing revival center. He loves to borrow a dirty Bethlehem stable and release through it the greatest

Gift the world has ever seen. God loves to use the "least of these" to do His work.

God is already manifesting His power in the earth, but I believe it is time for the Lord to release His power in not only in the third world countries but all over the earth. The day of the miraculous is now. It is time for the sick ones and the lame ones in your community and in mine to be completely healed and set free. It is time for those suffering from emotional and mental conditions to be restored. It is time for the children of God to be seen as people who walk in the authority and the power of their Almighty Father. It is time for our worship centers to become places where the lost and the broken can find hope, life, wholeness, peace, and restoration.

When the men and women in the upper room where baptized by the Holy Spirit, they were endued with power to do the very miracles that we have just mentioned. I don't know about you, but I believe God's Word is true. I believe it when it says in John 14:12 that we are going to be doing greater works than what Jesus accomplished during his earthly ministry. I believe that the power of God that is about to be unleashed on the earth in our day will be greater than anything the first century church experienced. We have been given the greater promise and so we should expect greater levels of power in our day. It is time to catch the vision of what The Lord wants to do in our day.

I believe that the restoration of His glory in the earth has already begun. We have entered into a new day in the Kingdom of God. One marked by the Kabod and the Shekinah fused together. We will experience the weighty honor of God in ways we have never experienced it before. We will also be equipped with new levels of God's miraculous gifts, and they will be a Shekinah sign to the lost. Many will see and believe.

Chapter Eight

Supernatural Spiritual Hunger

Crying Out for Something More.

There is an aspect about our modern day culture that is becoming more and more apparent all the time; and that is the level of supernatural and spiritual hunger in our society. If you visit your local bookstore today, you will find a large selection of books on spiritual matters from religion to the occult. The same is true at your local movie rental store; a large portion of new release movies today are supernatural or spiritual in nature. The appetite of today's society for the supernatural has intensified greatly in the past few years.

Titles such as "Harry Potter" are presently topping the charts both in book sales and in box office ticket sales. Why is this? I believe it is because our society is starving for supernatural things. They know that there is a reality out there that is greater than the limited natural reality that they live in, and they will look just about anywhere they can to find it.

Who is it that downloaded this spiritual hunger into our modern society? Did the devil do that? Is he the one who has caused the people of this earth to be so fascinated with supernatural things? I do not believe so. I do not believe that Satan can take the credit for this desire in our culture. I believe that God Almighty is the one that has placed this desire in the hearts and lives of people. The Lord has woven into the very fabric of mankind a yearning and a longing for the supernatural. Each one of us was born with a desire to know the things of the spirit realm. We are not only physical beings but we are also spiritual beings, and the spiritual part of our make-up longs for spiritual things. Deep calls out unto deep!

-God Given Supernatural Desire-

Not only were we born with a desire for supernatural things, but I also believe that we are living in an age where The Lord wants to release another spiritual awakening. The Lord is longing to pour out His Spirit on the earth, and so He has intensified the level of spiritual hunger on our generation. He is causing the hearts of mankind to long for something larger and more powerful than themselves.

Unfortunately, in recent years, the church has not had much to offer in the area of the supernatural. All across America, people step inside of our churches and instead of being impacted by supernatural things; they are greeted by religious, traditional people caught up in religious, traditional practices. They come looking for the power of God, but all they find at many local churches is philosophy and doctrine. So they turn to the sorcerers of our day; the psychics and the mediums, or to science fiction movies and books to satisfy their hunger for the supernatural.

Christians often attempt to offset these cultic practices by preaching against them or by going public and holding demonstrations against them. And though it is true that these things are cultic and from the enemy, the answer is not to get political and attack the counterfeit source that the enemy has set up. The answer is to display the true supernatural source, which of course is the power of God. When you read the New Testament, it is very clear that the Lord intended for His people to walk in the supernatural. His design for the body of Christ is to demonstrate the power of God through signs and wonders.

Unfortunately, our enemy, the devil, is a clever counterfeiter. He knows perfectly well that mankind is hungry for supernatural experiences. Satan also knows that this hunger comes from God and that it has the potential to lead great numbers of people to Salvation, and so the enemy has devised ways to fulfill that hunger with lies and deception. He does not want people to find the true source of supernatural authority. However, the best the devil can do is weakly counterfeit what is actually true. And though there is a level of true power present in these counterfeits, they can not even come close to comparing to the awesome, accurate, supernatural ability that the Lord possesses and desires to release onto the earth. Almighty God is the one who holds the true source of authority in both heaven and earth. And The Lord longs to utilize His people to demonstrate that power.

This brings us back to the Shekinah glory of God. As we learned in a previous chapter, the Shekinah is a "visible sign"; it is a demonstration of God's glory. It is something supernatural that people can see with their own eyes. The Lord's intention for His people is that we operate in His Shekinah glory, and in doing so, we can display the supernatural power of God in front of a hungry seeking world.

-We are Called to Be a Supernatural People-

For too many years we have believed that the supernatural aspects of God's kingdom were optional. For some reason we have allowed ourselves to believe that the only thing that is really necessary is salvation. The gifts of the Spirit and the supernatural are all perks, but they are not really necessary to our Christian life. Well, I choose to break away from this traditional mindset, and I want to tell you that in the coming season, your ministry will be very ineffective if you are not operating in both the gifts of the Spirit and in the supernatural. In fact, if we really evaluate the body of Christ today we can see that ordinary expository preaching alone is not cutting it any more. Churches who are not walking in the supernatural are finding it very difficult to reach their communities with the Gospel. Knowledge alone is not getting the job done. The world is not simply saying, "Teach me"; they are now shouting, "SHOW ME". It is not enough anymore to simply know about God, people want to experience Him and the demonstrations of His life-changing power.

-Experience Matters-

There is a great deal of controversy in the church today regarding experiential faith. It is not uncommon to hear ministers preach and teach that your experiences simply do not matter. They teach that you can't trust your experiences and that experiential faith is un-Biblical. I believe this teaching is one of the main reasons the church does not flow in the supernatural. In my opinion, this teaching is simply not true. Your experiences do matter.

It is true that sometimes people's experiences directly conflict with the Word of God, and in this case we need to be very clear that the Word of God should always take preeminence over the experiences of man. But some Christian leaders teach that we should put little stock in any spiritual experience regardless of how it measures up to God's Word. To throw out experiential faith all together, is like throwing out the baby with the bathwater. Spiritual experience is crucial to our faith as believers. In fact, if you show me a Christian whose life lacks true spiritual experience, then I will show you a Christian who struggles in the area of faith. Experience is a critical ingredient to building faith in your life. We must learn to trust the experiences that the Lord has given us.

For too many years the church has operating from an academic orientation. God wants to shift us from an academic orientation to a supernatural, spiritual orientation. Don't misunderstand me, there is nothing wrong with education; we all need to continue to learn as much as possible from the Word of God. The problem is when we become so academic that we begin to belittle the things of the Spirit.

2 Corinthians chapter 2 tells us that the things of the Spirit can only be understood by the Spirit. When we try and use our minds to grasp spiritual truths - we fall short. Often when we are unable to come to a mental conclusion regarding a spiritual matter, we will dismiss the matter all together or make light of it. This happens because we are uncomfortable engaging our spirit man in order to find the correct answer. The deeper issue is we don't trust our spirit man to make decisions for us. Most Christians have spent a great deal of time cultivating their academic understanding, but have spent very little time cultivating spiritual discernment.

I believe that God intended for His people to constantly grow and increase in spiritual gifts and abilities. Each generation should surpass the previous generation. There should be a noticeable increase in the area of spiritual gifts from one generation to another. And yet if this was the case, then the level of power and ability that was present in the first century church should not be a high point in church history, but should be merely a foundational point. Each generation following that first century church should have seen an increase in the things of the Spirit. And yet that is not the case.

Today we look back to the first century church with awe and wonder at what the Lord did through the people of that day. Somewhere along the way we dropped the proverbial ball. Somewhere between the first century church and our present time, the church took off the mantle of signs and wonders and replaced it with academia and control. Regardless of what generation dropped the ball, we must be the generation that picks it back up. We must surrender to the Lord and repent for the mistakes that generations past have made, and ask for His restoration power to come and restore back to us the supernatural giftings that the Lord intended for us to walk in all along.

The Bible says we have not because we ask not. It also say's that if we ask, it will be given to us. So it is time we stop analyzing the spirit realm and start operating in the spirit realm. And it all begins by simply asking. I believe that the Lord is more than ready to release the Shekinah back to His people. He is more than ready to display His supernatural, life changing power upon the earth, and He has chosen the people of God to be the earthen vessel that will demonstrate this glory.

As the people of God, we are standing at the proverbial fork in the road. The Lord is giving us the opportunity to walk in His manifest glory, but, we have a choice to make. It is a corporate choice and yet it is a personal choice as well. Many Christians will choose the road of comfort and walk away from this glorious opportunity. Yet there will be many who will choose the road less traveled and begin to seek the Lord for the supernatural, life changing Shekinah glory of God. Those that choose this road will face opposition and will find that it is not always an easy road to travel; yet if they truly commit to being a carrier of God's glory they will never regret their decision. What choice will you make?

Chapter Nine

Drilling the Wells of Glory

Establishing an Oasis of His Glory

On the night of October 11th, 2003 the Lord gave me a dream regarding the glory of God. The setting for the dream was the sanctuary of Springs Harvest Fellowship (Now Freedom Church) in Colorado Springs, CO where I attended church. As a member of the worship team, I was usually on the platform each week. In the dream I was also standing on the platform of our church and the congregation had just finished a time of worship. Our pastor, Dutch Sheets, had come to the front and was standing at the pulpit leading the congregation in prayer. As he was standing there, a large drill bit about 3 ½ feet in diameter came down from the ceiling and began to dig into the carpet and the foundation of the building.

I saw a man standing at the location where the drill went into the floor. He was a construction worker, dressed in overalls, a work shirt and a hard hat. He was looking up at the ceiling and giving directions to whoever was running the drill. He was saying things like "Keep it coming! That's good! OK, give me a little more now".

In my dream, I stepped down off the platform and asked this construction worker what He was doing. He told me that he and his crew were drilling a well of God's glory. I thought to myself, "This fellow is going to drill a hole in the middle of the sanctuary".

Strangely, the man in my dream looked familiar to me, so I asked him if he had ever attempted to drill a well in this church before or perhaps in the church I attended back in Oregon. He said that they have tried to drill in many churches all across the nation. I asked him why the past times didn't work. He said, "Once the drill starts to dig in, it always makes a mess. People do not like us messing up their church and so they ask us to stop."

He continued to say that when they are asked to stop drilling, they would pack up and move on to another location. He said that they no longer get offended, because they are asked to stop just about everywhere they go.

I wanted to know why people were so apposed to his work, so I questioned him on what the drilling would entail. He said that first they must drill through the foundation, and when they do, it will cause everything to shake. That which was built by God will be able to stand up to the shaking but that which was built by man will not be able to stand. He said, "Our intentions are not to knock down your structures, our intentions are simply to drill a well. But that which is built by man can not stand up to the drilling process."

He then said that after they drill through the foundations they hit the bedrock of man's agenda. He said that if they are not asked to stop because of the initial mess or because of the shaking, they're almost always asked to stop when man's agendas are disturbed.

I asked him how deep the well would be, and he said that, if they are allowed to drill, then this well will be very deep. He said that this was a glory well and they are always deep. He said, "We have drilled wells of visitation in the past that were not as deep because they were only to generate water for a certain period of time. This well, however, is a well of God's glory and so it needs to last for a long season and therefore must be very deep."

After the dream ended, I awoke and began to seek the Lord for more insight and information regarding what I had seen. Since that day, the Lord has showed me many things regarding the glory that He wants to bring to the body of Christ.

-Preparing for the Well-

The Lord truly is ready to drill deep wells of His glory in the earth. The question is where will they be drilled? The Lord has revealed to me that there will be many wells. He will drill all over the earth in several places on every continent. His desire is that a well of His glory be drilled in every region. As for where they will be drilled, they will be in locations where the Body of Christ has taken the necessary steps to prepare for them.

How do we prepare for a well of God's glory? First of all we must have a purpose for the water. Wells have an intended purpose. They are used to bring water to the surface for a particular reason. If you do not have a reason for the water, then you don't need a well. If you do not intend to use the glory of God to fulfill the purposes of God, then you should not expect the Lord to drill a glory well in your midst.

Many believers today are very well acquainted with the intentions and purposes of man but they are unacquainted with the intentions and purposes of God. There is a reason why God wants to restore David's fallen tent. There is a reason why God wants to pour out His Kabod and His Shekinah on the earth. If we are not aware of God's intentions for His glory, then we are not ready to receive this outpouring from God. We will study the purposes of God's glory in the next chapter, but let me wet your appetite a little. It has to do with reaching the lost.

The second way we can prepare for God's glory is by being willing to pay the price. In my dream, the "drill master" told me that they can't help but make a mess when they drill. Have you ever watched a drill as it digs into the earth? It pulls up dirt and mud from below the surface and lays it out on top the ground. It unearths things. Many of us have things in our lives that we have buried hoping to never have to see them again. But as the drill passes through those areas, it will pull up those things and lay them out on the surface where we have no choice but to deal with them.

Are you willing to deal with what the drill unearths? You never know what will be dug up until the drill starts digging. Are you willing to pay the price of dealing with the past? Will you allow God to dig up the unresolved areas of your life in order to make way for the well of His glory?

In the dream the drill master also told me that the drill would cause a great shaking and some structures would probably fall down. What will you do if you watch as some of your hopes, dreams and agendas that you have sacrificed great amounts of time and energy for, come crashing down around you? Will you get angry and tell God to stop drilling, or will you embrace the changes that God is bringing to your life? These are the price tags of the glory well.

The best way to tell God that you are willing to pay the price is by dying to yourselves. When we are dead, then our dreams and our visions are no longer important to us. When we truly surrender ourselves to the purposes of God, we are telling the Lord that we will not get offended if He rearranges a few things in our lives.

One thing that people fail to realize is that there are two parallel digs happening at the same time. Not only is the Lord digging a glory well corporately in fellowships and churches, He is also digging one in the individual lives of people. The body of Christ is made up of individual people. Many people are crying out for God's glory to come and visit their church buildings or their Sunday meetings, but I have news for them. God is not interested in putting a swimming pool in the "Amen Corner" of your church sanctuary so that you can come and splash in the water on Sunday morning; He is interested in digging a glory well in your heart. If you and those in your fellowship are not willing to allow the Lord to drill His well into your personal lives, than you will not be positioned to receive a corporate well of His glory. It all starts with the individual. You must first allow the Lord to drill in your heart and in your spirit.

-Whosoever Will May Come-

One of the questions we need to ask ourselves is what happens after the well is dug? Who will drink from it? The purpose of a well is to supply water for a specific reason, so who will this water be accessible to? I believe that the intention of a glory well is to have a place were men and women can come and freely partake of God's glory.

Up until the late 1800's, water was not automatically pumped into our homes, instead, men and women would bring their jars and containers out to the well and fill them up. They would then take the water home with them. In the wells of glory that God is digging in the earth, men and women will come not only to partake themselves but also to carry back a deposit of glory home with them to their families, their churches, and their communities.

The locations that are chosen to host a well of glory must be places that allow outsiders in. They must not be partial to who comes and partakes. They can not be places of prejudice. The Holy Spirit will draw all types of people to the well; we must be ready to embrace them all.

In Isaiah 55:1 it says,

"Come, all you who are thirsty, come to the waters; and you who have no money, come, buy and eat! Come buy wine and milk without money and without cost." (NIV)

The common paradigm in most churches and ministries is that we want The Lord to bring us healthy people who can help our ministries grow. We want to surround ourselves with people who are talented, or who have money and resources that will assist us in fulfilling our dreams and desires. There is nothing wrong with calling in resourceful people, but too often we forget that we are called to be a place of refuge for the poor and the hurting. I love this verse in Isaiah 55 because it puts everything back in the proper perspective. We need to be calling not only the talented and resourceful in, but we should also be calling anyone who is thirsty to come and drink, even if they appear to have nothing to give in return. The truth is they have more to offer than you know.

The tendency of the church is to try and protect or control any move of God that comes to her midst. As priests, we will be called to care and tend to the glory well of God, but we can never attempt to control it or mandate who comes to partake from it. The glory wells of God will be open to anyone who is thirsty, anyone who is longing for more of God, regardless of their history or their current position in life.

-Carry Home the Glory-

When we look at the Toronto outpouring we see a principle that is important to the coming wells of glory. As the news of the Toronto Blessing traveled around the world, men and women from every continent felt drawn to come and see what was going on. What happened after that is what is so important to us today. Many of those that went to Toronto were radically transformed by the great outpouring of the Father's love, and when they left Toronto, they actually carried home with them this renewal fire to their local churches. The local church then flowed in the same outpouring and manifestations that Toronto did. So much in fact that you no longer felt that you had to make the trip to Toronto in order to participate in the Toronto Blessing. It was as if the blessing had come to you. As this continued to happen, Toronto actually started calling their conferences "Catch the Fire". The meaning being that you could actually go and catch the fire and take it back home with you.

I believe the coming wells of Glory will have the same transferring ability. Many will come to the wells and be radically changed, and something will be deposited into them that they can actually take home and utilize to impact their local areas. And just as Toronto has been and still is willing and faithful to host the well of God's renewal, so you and I must be willing and faithful to host a well of God's glory.

The Lord is looking for sacrificial houses of hospitality that will welcome weary travelers, have a passion and a desire to see them radically changed, and send them home with the ability to transform their local communities.

So the next time God moves in your midst and it looks like things are getting a little too messy for your comfort level, just calm down and go with it. If you see some of your hopes and dreams start to shake at their very foundations, just relax. The drill has begun to turn. Your destiny is not in jeopardy. In fact your destiny has just begun to be fulfilled. It may not look like the destiny that you planned for yourself, but it is the destiny that you were chosen for. You are destined to be a priest before the glory of God. Allow the Lord's drill to dig deep into your life. And as you do, watch as the Lord begins to also dig deep into your church body. And before long the Lord will establish a well of His manifest glory that will bubble up in the midst of His people, and many will come and partake and be transformed by the power of God.

Chapter Ten

The Purposes of His Glory

Discovering God's Motive for Releasing His Glory

Most of us, at one time or another has asked God the "Why" question. A couple examples of the "why" question might be, "Lord, why have I not received my healing yet?" or, "Father, Why don't you answer my prayers?" We want to know why God allows us to face certain things in our lives. Maybe, you have asked Him to intervene in a particular area of your life, and it doesn't appear that He is doing so. Or maybe your family has faced a difficult trial and you find yourself wondering "why". We are a very inquisitive people. It is not enough to just know "what" is happening to us, we have to know "why" it is happening. Even when the good things happen to us, often we find ourselves wondering why.

Well, how about this question, "Why restore David's tent?", or "Why dig wells of glory in the earth?" If you are like me you have to know why. You find yourself wondering what the Lord's intentions are for restoring His glory to the earth. There are several purposes that we could discuss, but I want to take a moment and discuss the three that I believe are His key purposes.

First of all, I believe that the Lord wants to restore David's tent for the purpose of restoring intimacy with His children. As we discussed in an earlier chapter, the heart of God longs for intimacy with you and me. He wants to be near us. He wants to communicate with us, and He wants to lavish His blessings upon us. He has a passion for us that is greater than our finite minds can conceive. But just like any loving relationship, love must flow both ways. We too must be passionately in love with Him. We must long for intimacy with God the same way that He longs for intimacy with us. One sided relationships never work.

-Sharing God's Passion-

Have you ever noticed how passionate you can get about the things that matter to your loved ones? For instance, your wife or husband may have a particular passion that you never really thought too much about, but now that you are married to that individual, their passions seemed to have worn off on you. You find yourself caring about the same things they care about.

For example, my wife, Kathleen, is part Irish and has a passion for Ireland. In fact, her sister and brother-in-law are presently serving as missionaries to Northern Ireland. She has always wanted to vacation there and perhaps even minister there someday. Ireland has never been a vacation dream of mine, but now that I am married to her I have truly caught her Irish bug. Now, I too find myself wanting to vacation there, and we are actually planning to go and visit her family in Ireland next year.

If each of us took a moment and thought about it, we could all come up with areas that we now care about because we have caught someone else's vision. In the same way, God wants us to become passionate about the things that He is passionate about. God wants to transfer the cares of His heart to us. But before we can truly have the heart of God we must be intimate with Him. God wants to pour out His glory in such a way that we fall in love with Him all over again. He wants to give us His heart. He wants us to burn with passion for the things that He is passionate for. I believe the glory will bring a new level of intimacy with God, because as we draw near to His glory we will come to know His heart.

Another key purpose for the release of God's glory in our day is to empower the saints. I believe we are entering into a season where all the saints will regularly heal the sick, and raise the dead. For the past several years the church has set back and let their big name pastors, evangelists, and missionaries, be the ones to actually operate in the miraculous giftings of God. We can no longer afford to leave all the supernatural work of God for a hand full of gifted missionaries and evangelists to do. There is simply too much work that needs to get done. It is time for the body of Christ to rise up and lay hold of its full inheritance. We need all the saints (Yes that means you) to step up to the plate and pick up the mantle of the miraculous.

The Bible tells us that signs and wonders should follow those who believe in the Lord. The Lord longs to heal, deliver, and set free. We are called to be the hands and feet that carry the miraculous to those who are broken and dying in our world.

God wants to empower us. His Word tells us that we are to be imitators of Christ. We are to actually look like and act like the Lord. The Lord was a miracle worker, and if we are to act and look like Him, it is necessary that we have the same miraculous power of God working through us.

-It's All About The Lost-

Thirdly, I believe the primary key purpose for God's glory being restored to the earth today is to usher in the harvest. God's heart has always been for the lost. The Lord's desire is that none perish and that all come to repentance in Christ Jesus. When the Lord pours out His glory on the earth it accomplishes many things, but its main purpose is to see the lost come to know the Lord.

Let's take a closer look at Amos 9. We have already looked at verse eleven and learned that God will restore David's tent to our generation, but when we look at the next few verses that follow we see why God wants to restore the tabernacle of David.

Verse 13 says,

"The days are coming" declares the Lord, "when the reaper will be overtaken by the plowman and the planter by the one treading grapes. New wine will drip from the mountains, and flow from all the hills." (NIV)

This verse speaks of the harvest. In fact it speaks of such a great harvest that the planting is not even finished before the harvest is ripe and ready to be harvested. This verse is what I like to call a paradigm shifter. It forces you to change what you have always believed about the Harvest. It replaces the old model where some plant, others water and some bring in the harvest, with a brand new model where the planting, watering and harvesting are all done simultaneously. This verse speaks of a harvest that is so great and so quick that there is not time to do things the old conventional way.

Why does God want to restore David's tent in this generation? I believe it is because God wants to usher in a great harvest in our day. We have already learned that the Shekinah glory is the visible sign of His presence. It is not a sign to the believer; it is a sign to the lost. God wants to send a visual message to the lost declaring and demonstrating how much He loves them. He wants to reveal to the lost that He is real. He wants to show your unsaved loved ones that the Gospel is true. And He will do this with signs and wonders, through the outpouring of His glory.

What do signs do? They give us direction and instruction. They give us a "heads up" of what is coming. Signs keep us from getting lost. They show us which way is the right way. Just as natural signs point us in the correct direction so the glory of God works as a sign to the unbeliever, pointing the lost in the direction of the cross.

There are many times throughout the Old Testament where God revealed His glory to the children of Israel. Each time He did, it always brought repentance of sin and new dedication to the will of the Lord. There was always a refocusing and a returning to the things of God with every display of His glory. Even in the New Testament when Jesus demonstrated the glory of God through miracles, many would believe in Him and follow Him.

As priests before the glory of God, we must also share the Father's heart for the lost. We must have a passion and a desire to see the lost come to know the Lord. Many churches today are not reaching out to the lost to the degree that they should. They have become so inward focused on their programs and the workings of the church that outreach has become simply an 'add on', or a secondary ministry of the church.

If your local fellowship is to be selected as a location for one of God's glory wells, then as a fellowship, you are going to have to shift your focus back to one of our original purposes; The great commission. If you are to truly host the glory of God, you must have a burning desire within you to see the lost saved. And that desire needs to be followed up by action. Many people may say that they want to see the lost saved, but they are not actively involved in making that happen. The Bible tells us that faith without works is dead faith.

-Time Sensitive Business-

Harvesting is a time sensitive business. When I was a child, our family would plant a large garden every year on my Grandmother's property. We would grow tomatoes, corn, green beans, peppers, zucchini, and carrots to name a few. Each vegetable would ripen at a different time than the other vegetables. If you tried to harvest them too early you would end up with vegetables that were not quite as sweet as they could have been. However, if you waited too long to harvest them, they would become over-ripe and risked becoming infested with bugs and worms. There was a precise timing to harvesting the vegetables.

Besides harvesting there was a process that must be followed after the harvest was done. It was not enough to simply pick the tomatoes; you had to have a plan for them. They had to be canned or eaten before they went bad. The point is you had to be ready for the harvest.

We must be ready for the harvest of souls that God is about to bring us. It will not be enough to simply lead them through the sinner's prayer. We must have a plan to teach, disciple and train them. We have to be prepared in advance before the harvest time begins.

The glory will attract all kinds. There will be the lost that have no understanding of God at all, but when they come into contact with His glory they will desire to know the Lord. There will be the prodigals who have been a part of Father's house in the past but have allowed their faith to grow cold. They will come back to the Lord when they see the Shekinah fire of God alive in the body of Christ. There will also be the hurting and the broken believers, who have been wounded by the church in the past. They will come hoping for answers and looking for healing. We must be ready to embrace all of these.

Harvest time is upon us and if we will diligently prepare for it then the Lord will pour out His glory in an unprecedented way. As He does, we will see many wonderful things happen. The Shekinah will once again show the lost the saving power of God.

Chapter Eleven

Preparing For His Glory

*Properly Positioning Ourselves
for the Coming Move of God*

For many years now I have been carrying around a burden for the outpouring of God's glory. Everywhere I go there are two questions that people ask in regards to this subject. First of all, "What do we do in order to prepare for His glory?" And second, "What will it look like when God's glory comes in its fullness?" I am not sure that I or anyone else can fully answer the second question until we actually experience the fullness of His glory. But we can locate some information in regards to the first question by studying some of the outpourings of God's glory in the Bible.

There are several places in the Bible where God's glory appeared to man. Each time the lives of men and women were radically changed. I want us to take a second look at two examples in scripture where the glory appeared and what preparations took place leading up to them.

-Interrupted by His Glory-

The first example I want us to look at is Solomon's Temple. 1 Kings Chapter 8 tells us that after the Temple was built, the priest brought the Ark of the Covenant in and placed it inside the Holy of Holies. Verse 10 tells us that as they withdrew themselves from the Holy Place the cloud (or Kabod) of God filled the Temple of the Lord. We read in the next verse that the priests were unable to perform their duties because the glory of God was so thick in the temple. When you study the Kabod of God in scripture there is one thing that you see every time; it always stopped people in their tracks. It always demanded their attention.

I Kings Chapter 8 tells us that the priests were not able to perform their duties because of the mighty presence of God. When was the last time you could not perform your duties in church because of God's glory? Most of us could look back over our entire Christian lives and never come up with an answer.

What would it have been like to stand there at Solomon's temple and to behold the presence of God in such a way that it stopped you in your tracks? It must have been awesome. One true sign of the Kabod in our day is that it will interrupt our schedule.

-Ask the Lord for Strategy-

Let's look at what led up to the Kabod of God falling in Solomon's temple. The construction of Solomon's Temple was quite an undertaking. Thirty thousand men were sent to Lebanon in shifts of 10,000 men per month, to cut down cedar trees to be used in the construction of the Temple. The cedar lumber was then floated on rafts from Lebanon to Israel. There were 80,000 stonecutters sent to the hills to quarry the stones that would be used in the construction of the Temple. There were 70,000 men whose assignment was to simply carry all the wood and stones. There were over 3,300 foremen who supervised the construction.

The fine details that Solomon used in the temple were very intricate. The walls were made of fine quarried stone, there was ornately carved cedars fitted into the structure. Artists carved cherubim on the interior walls of the temple. The floors were covered with gold and polished so brightly that your reflection shined back up at you.

The point that I want us to see here is that there was a divine plan that had to be followed before the glory was released. Things had to be in place. The Lord showed Solomon how to prepare for His glory.

And when Solomon was faithful to follow God's divine strategy, then God released His glory. As we prepare for our own release from God, we too must be deliberate about following the plans that God gives us. God is constantly releasing strategy to His people. We should be quick to ask the Lord for His divine strategy. Some times that strategy is received through prayer, other times it is received through the illumination of the written Word, and other times it comes by way of the prophetic. Regardless of how God releases strategy to us, we must be diligent to follow it.

-Count the Cost-

Another thing we can learn from Solomon's temple is the cost of hosting the glory of God. You can easily see how it cost Solomon a great deal before the glory came, but what you may not know is how much it continued to cost him after the glory arrived. As you read on in 1 Kings 8 you see that after the glory of God had come, there was a great sacrifice that took place. Verse 63 tells us that King Solomon gave the Lord a sacrifice of fellowship offerings. The Bible says that 22,000 cattle and 120,000 sheep and goats were sacrificed to the Lord in the outer courts.

We have already spoken of the sacrifice that the Lord requires prior to the outpourings of His glory, but here in 1 Kings 8 we learn that the sacrifices didn't end after the glory showed up. In fact the greatest sacrifice took place after the glory came. Hosting a glory well will not be cheap. It is a sacrificial calling that must be taken seriously. There is a price to pay to host God's manifest glory.

You can expect your old schedules and time commitments to change when the glory of God arrives. I believe that once the Kabod and Shekinah are released in their fullness, they will draw people like steel to a magnate. People will come from all over the area desperate for the things of God. As priests we are called to facilitate this outpouring. This will not be a Sunday only responsibility. Expect your schedule to change drastically.

-One Mindset and One Passion-

The other example I want us to look at is found in the outpouring of God's glory on the Day of Pentecost. We have already studied the similarities between the Day of Pentecost and the Old Testament tabernacles. We have discerned how the Kabod of God came in and deposited the Shekinah. We also have discovered what happened after the Shekinah came; how the 120 believers left the upper room and carried the miraculous into the earth.

I want us to take a serious look at the days leading up to Pentecost. How did they prepare for such a historical visitation of God? What can we learn as we await our own visitation?

Acts 2:1 says.

"When the day of Pentecost had fully come, they were all with one accord in one place."(NKJV)

When you study the word "accord" in the Greek you find that the meaning of this word is: *"with one mindset or with one passion"*. What this is saying is that once they were in one place with one mindset and one passion then suddenly the Glory of God came.

So often when we come together as a body of believers to worship, we find ourselves in one place but unfortunately not in one accord. We are not there with one passion and one mindset. All too often each of us comes with our own agendas, our own paradigms and our own opinions. On the day of Pentecost there was a unity that bonded the group together. They each desired the same thing. They were longing and waiting for the outpouring of the Holy Spirit.

I believe that they were probably not all in one accord when they first came together in the upper room, but after 10 days of waiting on the Lord together, their passions and mindsets began to unify. They did not receive their open Heaven until they were united with one mind and one passion.

We too need an open Heaven in our day. Could it be that the same key that unlocked the doors of Heaven on the Day of Pentecost is the key that we need today? Yes, I believe so. We must come together in unity of mind and passion if we want to see the Lord pour out His glory.

I have heard it taught that a great multitude was present the day that Jesus ascended in the clouds into heaven; at least 500 men not including women and children. If this is true, then a large number of people heard Jesus tell them to go to Jerusalem and wait for Him to send the Holy Spirit.

Yet on the day of Pentecost there were only 120 people in the upper room. So what happened to everyone else? Did they get tired of waiting? It had only been 10 days since Jesus ascended to Heaven, was that too long to wait for the promises of God? Well Acts 2 sheds a little more light on this mystery by telling us that this happened early in the morning. So perhaps we can assume that the 120 people in the upper room that morning were the night watchmen. They were responsible to keep watch through the night.

Whatever the reason, only 120 people were present when the Holy Spirit fell. Why would God choose the early morning hours to pour out His Spirit? Why did He choose to pour out His Spirit on a mere 120 people? I personally believe it was because the larger group of 500 had not yet reached a place of "one accord" in the Spirit. But on that 10th morning of this nonstop prayer meeting, 120 people entered into a place of synergistic prayer where they were truly united in mindset and passion, and that unity was the key that God was waiting for. And in that place of unity, God released His Spirit.

Sometimes the Lord will allow our numbers to diminish for our own good. Often we think that there is greater power in larger numbers, but God knows who needs to be present. He knows the ones who will walk together in unity of purpose. He doesn't need a multitude; He loves to work with a remnant.

It doesn't take a multitude to usher in the glory of God. It only takes the few that will answer the priestly call and wait for His promises. When the 120 left the upper room that day, little did they know that the message that they were about to share would radically transform the world. They were only a small band of people, yet they were about to preach and teach the greatest truth the world would ever hear. As we prepare for the coming outpouring of God's glory we must be in one accord with the Spirit of God. If each of us is in one accord with the Spirit of God, then we will also be in one accord with each other.

There is a specific time when God will release His glory into our midst. It will be at a Kairos moment. And just like in Solomon's temple or Pentecost's upper room, when it comes it will stop us in our tracks and demand our attention.

I believe that we have everything we need in order for God to move. We are not waiting on God to release something more from the Heavens in order for us to see His glory. He has already equipped us with all the necessary pieces to the puzzle. He is also in the process of gathering all the right people. Now is the time to put the pieces and the people together. When everything is in its place, and the people are in one accord then we will see the outpouring of the glory of God. I believe that day is soon.

Chapter Twelve

Truck Drivers Wanted

*Carriers of His Glory That are
Not Afraid to Go the Distance*

Almost every one of us at one time or another has picked up the Sunday paper and perused through the classifieds looking for that perfect job. Have you ever noticed that certain jobs seem to always be in the paper? You know which ones I am talking about; they are the jobs that you are not qualified to apply for. The one ad that never fails to show up when I look at the paper is, "Truck Drivers Wanted". No matter what paper I read that ad is almost always there.

What if God had a newspaper? What ads would He put in His classified section? I wonder if God's Sunday paper would run a *"Truckers Wanted"* ad.

I believe that He would. Why do I believe this? It is because God needs people who know how to go the distance. God is looking for some long haulers who will carry out the work of the Lord.

-Trucking for the Lord-

In October of 2000, while visiting the World Prayer Center in Colorado Springs, the Lord gave me a dream about trucks, truckers and the glory of God. The World Prayer Center has beautiful, hotel-style rooms called 'prayer rooms' where you can spend the night. It was while I was staying in one of these prayer rooms that the Lord gave me this dream. God used this dream to show me once again that this is the generation that will see the rebuilding of David's tent.

The dream was centered on a large moving truck. The back of the truck was full of building tools. Some were old outdated hand tools that did not require electricity to use. These tools were well worn. They were still usable, but it would take much time and effort if they were the only tools you had to work with. These tools were all hanging on the left side of the truck.

On the right side of the truck, however, were Brand new precision power tools that did require electricity to operate. Once they were plugged in and powered up, they had the ability to get the job done quickly and accurately. All the tools in the truck were construction tools that you would use in building homes and other buildings. In my dream, however, I knew that these tools were not for the constructing of homes, but for the re-building of David's fallen tent.

As the dream continued I found myself backing up this moving truck to my home church at that time. In 2000 my home church was South Lane Christian Center in Cottage Grove, Oregon. The Pastors and elders from the different churches around town came together and carried a large spool of power cord out to the truck. They attached the spool to the back of the truck and then unwound just enough power cord to allow them to plug me into one of the church's power outlets. I immediately realized that this power cord would provide the necessary electricity I needed to run the precision tools in the back of the truck.

The pastors then prayed for me and sent me out to minister to the body of Christ. The cable was long enough to reach anywhere I wanted to go in the regional area. In my dream I could see myself driving all over the area. I ministered in worship and then began calling believers to rise up and re-build David's tent in their region. After ministering all over the area, I tried to head up the interstate so I could minister in other communities and states to the north. I remember thinking how great it would be to minister all over Oregon, Washington, and even British Columbia. Unfortunately I was on too short of a leash. I ran out of power cord as I tried to leave the regional area where I was plugged in at. I would still be able to minister but I would have to rely on the old hand tools to do so.

I woke up from the dream and immediately realized that God was trying to speak to me. I laid there in bed and started to pray for the meaning of the dream. However, since I did not get out of bed, it wasn't 5 minutes later and I was back to sleep without an answer to my prayer. Oddly enough, as soon as I fell back asleep, the dream started all over again.

The second dream was almost identical to the first dream except for the location. Instead of backing up the moving truck to my home church in Cottage Grove, Oregon, this time I was backing up to the city of Colorado Springs, Colorado. Again the local pastors and elders (this time from Colorado Springs) came and attached a large spool of power cord to the back of the truck. They plugged me in and covered me in prayer just like the pastors had done in Cottage Grove. They then sent me out to minister to the body of Christ. The difference this time, though, was there was no limit to the power cord on the truck. I could go anywhere in the nation or even to other nations. Anywhere the road would take me I was able to go.

I woke up again and realized that the Lord was obviously trying to speak to me. So this time I got out of bed and began to seek the Lord for the meaning of these two dreams. The Lord spoke to me very specifically. He told me that for the last several years He had called me to minister in Cottage Grove, and that I was to continue to minister there, but the day would come when He would call me to Colorado Springs, and when He called, I was not to hesitate but to go immediately.

-Mantles of Authority-

When I asked the Lord about the power cables, He told me that He gives mantles of authority to us at different times in our lives. He also told me that there are regional mantles placed over different cities. He told me that to the believers in Cottage Grove He had given the mantle of reaching its entire region with the Gospel, building up the body of Christ and establishing the Kingdom of God in that area. With those mantles comes the authority to dispel the darkness and bring the light of Christ to the lost.

The Lord then told me that because the local body has been faithful to the mantles that He had given them, He is adding greater mantles of authority to them, and that their power cords will continue to stretch further and further. He said that He is mobilizing the saints in that region to fulfill the call that He has given them. He spoke with such love and fondness for the local church that I began to understand the great calling and authority that God had given this faithful body of believers. The Lord continued to say that as I plug into that mantle I will have the authority to do the work that that mantle holds.

He then said that, "to the believers in Colorado Springs I have also given mantles of authority. The mantle I have given to that city is not only to reach its region but to reach the nation and the world. This is why I have based so many national and international ministries there."

He told me that there are key cities around the world that He has cloaked with national and international authority, and that Colorado Springs is one of those cities. The Lord told me that He is calling many people to plug into Colorado Springs. As they do, they will carry the authority of that mantle and He will thrust them out into the earth to build the Kingdom in the places that He directs. Seven months later the Lord moved me to Colorado Springs.

I spent three years and three months in Colorado. During that time the Lord plugged me into the ministry of Springs Harvest Fellowship (Now Freedom Church) where Apostle Dutch Sheets is the pastor. After three years there, Springs Harvest ordained me as a minister of their fellowship and released me to move to South Dakota to minister in worship and help dig wells of God's glory in the Midwest. The morning of my ordination, was the same day that my wife Kathleen and I were to leave for South Dakota. One thing that I find awesome and yet humorous is that I had a moving truck parked out in the church parking lot on the day that I got ordained (plugged in) by Springs Harvest.

The reason I shared this story with you is not to entice you to move to Cottage Grove or Colorado Springs, but to show you that God is indeed mobilizing His people. God has given mantles of authority to every believer, every family, every church and every city. As faithful members of the local body, we need to continue to faithfully fulfill the call that God has given us.

God is about to pour out His glory in the earth. I believe that He will drill initial wells of glory in several key locations around the world. But God's intent is not that His glory be displayed only in those locations. He wants His Glory to spread into the whole earth. So what is it going to take to spread the glory of God? It is going to take Priests who will plug in to those glory wells and then get in their moving trucks and carry that glory out into the earth. The Lord will not allow His glory to be contained or confined within one locality; He wants it taken out into the communities and into the marketplaces. God is indeed looking for some priestly truck drivers who will be willing to go the distance regardless of the cost.

-Equipped for the Call-

God wants to equip us to do the work that He has called us to do. In my dream there were tools lining the walls of the moving truck. Tools speak of equipping. God wants to equip us with the proper tools so that we can prepare places for God's glory to come and dwell.

In the dream there were two types of tools. On one side of the truck, there were old out dated tools that were well worn. These tools could still be used, but if they were the only tools you had to work with, then you progress would be slowed down considerably. On the other side of the truck were precision power tools that had the ability to do the job not only quickly, but more importantly, with precise accuracy.

I believe that God wants to give us new tools for the work that He is calling us to do. If we try to use the old tools that God gave us during our past revivals, we will slow down the process tremendously. I believe that God is calling us to do a quick work. Therefore, He is in the business of re-equipping us with the proper tools to get the job done.

The day of God's glory is now. We are not talking about an outpouring that will take place years down the road. The Lord is ready to pour Himself out in our day. We must prepare the way for the coming outpouring of His glory.

It takes a special kind of person to be a truck driver. The hours are long. The road is even longer. You are always on the move. You find yourself in places that are miles away from home. You don't see your family as much as you would like. Yet there are those that have the grace to do this kind of work; for they love the open road and they are not afraid to go the distance.

Evangelists and Missionaries are in some ways spiritual truck drivers. They are called to travel to far away towns, cities, and nations and proclaim the message of Christ. As priests before the Lord, we too

Gathering the Priests

are called to carry out the glory of God into the earth. The Lord is looking for priests who are not afraid to go out where the lost are and show them the power of God's glory.

God is currently drilling wells. He is doing so in various places in the earth. He is also rising up and equipping priests. Are you one of those truck-drivers being divinely prepared by God? Is there a stirring inside of you to go out to the weary people of your area and see them restored and healed? If so, then maybe you are in God's truck-driving school right now. Maybe you are being prepared to be a holy trucker who will go the distance for the cause of His glory.

-Willingness is the Key-

The question is, "Are you willing to answer the call?" All it takes is a willing heart. God isn't looking for the most eloquent speakers, or the most charismatic, dashing leaders to answer the priestly call. He is simply looking for willing people.

If you know anything at all about truck drivers, you know that they do not need to have their masters or doctorate degree in transportation in order to perform their profession. They don't have to be great public speakers, or have great charisma. They only have to be ready to go the distance, and be willing to receive the proper training to do the task that is set before them.

If you are willing to go the distance, then you are exactly the candidate that God is looking for. The Lord doesn't choose the noble or the wise, he chooses the willing. That is the primary prerequisite for being selected as a modern day priest.

So I ask you again, are you willing? Does your heart long for people to be changed by the manifest glory of God? If it does, then ask the Lord to give you a new mantle. Ask Him to equip you with the right tools to become a carrier of His glory. Willingness is the key.

Chapter Thirteen

Always Read the Safety Labels

The Danger Zones of Being a Priest

Many years ago, I worked as the custodial manager at a compact disc manufacturing plant in Oregon. As a custodian, I was accustomed to using multiple types of cleaning chemicals designed for different purposes around the plant. Some were for general cleaning such as hard surfaces and floors. Others had specific purposes and were used to clean particular machines and objects inside the plant. But regardless of what their purposes were, they all had safety labels on the side of the bottle. Some safety labels read, "Avoid contact with eyes." Others read, "Harmful if swallowed." Still others read, "CAUTION: Highly Corrosive, Avoid Contact with Skin."

Gathering the Priests

The purpose of these safety labels was to give you an advance warning of the harm that the chemical can cause. As a custodian I was taught to always read the safety labels.

Many things have safety labels. Lawn mowers have warnings and safety instructions on them. Power tools also have safety labels. Each is designed to inform us of a present danger that can occur if you use the tool incorrectly.

When it comes to the things of God, I believe the Bible gives us some clear safety labels that we must make sure we know before we attempt to carry and/or handle the glory of the Lord. To find these safety labels in scripture, we need to study those who mishandled God's glory and paid a heavy price for it.

First, let's take another look at David's attempts to bring the Ark of the Covenant back to Jerusalem. In an earlier chapter, we studied David's two attempts in great detail. The first attempt ended in utter failure. That is the one I want to take a second look at.

If you remember, the Ark of the Lord had been in the border town of Kirjath Jearim at the home of Abinadab for 20 years. Abinadab had two sons, Uzzah and Ahio. These two boys had literally grown up with the Ark in their home and were very accustomed to having it around.

As we have already studied, David went to the home of Abinadab with a new cart to carry it back to Jerusalem. During the journey, Ahio would go before the ark and Uzzah was to follow right behind it. When they reached Nachan's threshing floor the cart hit a bump and the Ark began to teeter. Uzzah, not wanting the Ark to fall off the cart, reached up and steadied it. And when He did, God burned with anger toward Uzzah and struck him dead.

What would the safety label be in this example? I believe it would read like this; "Touch not the holy things of God." It could also read, "Do not take the glory of God for granted." Uzzah had grown up around the Ark and he had grown too accustomed to it. He took it for granted and therefore had lost any fear or reverence for it. As modern day Priests, we need to make sure we never come to a place where we take God's glory for granted. The quickest way to shut down the anointing is to touch the holy things of God.

I believe that another problem Uzzah struggled with was pride. He may have seen this day as his day to shine in the spot light. His family was the only one in all of Israel that had any recent history with this ancient artifact. It had been in their home for the past twenty years and no one else had access to it. Now he and his brother were the ones selected to march in the processional. Could it be that Uzzah saw this as "his chance to be somebody"? Uzzah could have easily become arrogant about his position in the parade. Unfortunately, his pride caused him to be stupid, and his stupidity cost him his life.

There are many Uzzahs alive in the church today. Maybe they have been given a spiritual gift or a special anointing. They have operated in their gift for so long, that they now see it as "*their* gift" not "*God's* gift". They have built their identity around the anointing that God has given them. As far as they are concerned they are something special because of the much needed gifts that they possess. They want people to see them as "Brother Wonderful", or "Sister Anointed". However, if they are not careful, they can become a modern day Uzzah. They can take for granted the things of the Lord.

When the glory of God begins to deposit the miraculous into each of us, we must be very careful that we do not see ourselves as better than others or greater than most. We must always remember it is the Lord's power and not ours that we operate in. If we loose sight of that truth, we can become blinded just like Uzzah did.

Another Biblical example where we can find a safety label regarding the glory of God is in the account of Ananias and Sapphira. The glory had been poured out at the Day of Pentecost and now, only a short time later, the story of Ananias and Sapphira takes place.

All the Christians of the early church believed that none of their possessions were their own. They shared everything they had. They would sell their lands and their goods and bring the proceeds to the local body of believers so that they could give to those in need. Acts 4:32 says the believers were all one in heart and mind on this matter.

A man named Ananias together with his wife Sapphira also sold a piece of land. They told the leaders that they were selling it for the work of the Kingdom, but instead of bringing the whole profits of the sale to give to the Kingdom, they kept a part back for themselves. Ananias then told Peter that they had given the entire sale to the work of God.

Peter, knowing that Ananias was lying, confronted him. He asked Ananias why he would lie to God. When Ananias heard what Peter said, he fell dead on the ground. They carried him out and buried his body. His wife Sapphira came to Peter about three hours later. She too was asked if the money they had given to the Lord was the entire sale of the property. Not knowing what had happened to her husband, she immediately said it was. Again Peter confronted her for lying to God. She too fell dead. They carried her out and buried her by her husband.

What is the safety label here? After the glory of God comes in its fullness we will not be allowed to live a life of false pretense in front of each other. Priests must be truthful and real. The days of getting away with being fake and phony are over. We must be speakers of truth. The safety label on God's glory may read something like this; "Caution: The Glory always exposes the truth, avoid contact with dishonesty."

Another Safety Label in Scripture that I believe we should address has to do with our priestly call. In 1 Samuel 2, we read about the priest Eli and his two sons Hophni and Phinehas. Eli was the high priest and his two sons were his apprentices. The Bible says that Hophni and Phinehas were wicked men. They mishandled the sacrifices that were brought to the temple. They would take the choices cuts of meat from the sacrifice and keep them for themselves as food. This was clearly disobedient to the Levitical code the Lord had given the priests. They were also promiscuous men. In 1 Samuel 2, we read that they slept with various women. They sinned greatly in the eyes of God.

In the Old Testament times, the office of the priest was one of position and authority. Eli's sons were clearly looked at as leaders in the nation. Because of their position, no one dare question them. Hophni and Phinehas took advantage of this for their own selfish gain. 1 Samuel tells us that Eli knew of his son's wrong doing yet did nothing about it. The Bible tells us that God's judgment burned not only toward Hophni and Phinehas but also against Eli because He did not correct the actions of his sons.

I believe that there are two safety labels here for us to look at. The first one is, "Never use your positions, giftings, and callings for selfish gain." Priests must be selfless. Once we allow selfishness to creep into our hearts we risk the same fate as Hophni and Phinehas.

Another safety label we can learn from this example is, "Never look the other way to avoid confrontation with sin." Eli knew his son's were involved in evil practices, but he chose to look the other way instead of confronting his son's about their actions. God's judgment was just as severe with Eli as it was with Hophni and Phinehas. We must not allow sin to remain unchecked in our hearts or in the hearts of those that we are called to lead.

God's holiness always accompanies His glory. We must not allow ourselves to ever become so accustomed to the things of God that we begin take them for granted. We also must never misuse God's gifts and callings for our own gain. God still has a standard that He requires of His priests and as the priests to our generation; we must be willing to embrace the standard that God has for those who carry His glory.

Chapter Fourteen

Joining the Remnant of Priests

It Only Takes a Remnant to Accomplish the Purposes of God

Throughout the Bible there is story after story where God took a small band of people and did mighty things through them. God always had a remnant. He did not need the world's greatest army or strongest nation to fulfill His purposes. God only needed a small group of sold-out radicals who were not afraid to trust the Lord regardless of how impossible the odds seemed.

There are many examples of God's chosen remnant in the scriptures, but one of my favorite ones is the story of Gideon's army. I want us to take a few moments and review this story because I believe the peculiar way that God selected His remnant for that historic battle is similar to the way He will select His remnant of priests for this generation.

The armies of Midian and Amelek had joined their forces together and were planning an attack against the nation of Israel. They had set up camp in the valley of Moreh. Judges 7 tells us that their joint forces were so large that they resembled a large swarm of locusts filling the entire valley. Judges 7:12 tells us that their camels alone were so many they could not be counted.

In the nearby hill country of Mount Gilead, Gideon, along with thirty-three thousand men, was camped out at the spring of Harod. In Judges 7:2 God told Gideon something that seemed ridiculous; He said that Gideon had too many men. God said that He didn't need that many men to defeat the Midianites and the Amelekites. He told Gideon that some of the men should go home. Now, if I were Gideon I would be telling God to go back and check His math. Gideon's mind must have been spinning as he thought of going to war against the countless thousands down in the enemy camp with his small group of only 33,000 men. And yet the Lord said that there were simply too many men. The Lord said to send away anyone who was fearful. So being obedient to God, Gideon pulled the men together and told them that if they were fearful they should leave. Twenty-three thousand men packed up and headed for home.

Now, Gideon had only ten thousand men left. Again, God told Gideon that there were too many men. This time the Lord directs Gideon to take the men to the river and have everyone take a drink. He said that while they are at the river He would sort out the men that were to continue from the ones that were to leave. So Gideon took the men to the river to drink.

Everyone took a drink. Nine thousand, seven hundred of them knelt down and put their faces in the water to drink. Judges 7:5 says that three hundred of them cupped the water with their hands and then lapped the water out of their hands with their tongues like dogs. The Lord told Gideon to send everyone home except for the three hundred.

So Gideon's Army shrunk from thirty-three thousand down to only three hundred men. And now, a small remnant was all that was left to fight the joint forces of the Midianites and the Amelekites. How do you win a war against tens of thousands of troops when all you have to work with is a mere three-hundred men? It is seemingly impossible. Yet with God, all things are possible.

As this historical account unfolds, we see that God knew how to use sound effects and theatrical props long before Hollywood did. The three hundred man remnant would put on a theatrical performance that even Broadway could be proud of. Each of the men would carry three props; a trumpet, a torch, and an empty jar.

The three hundred were divided into three groups. In the middle of the night they quietly snuck their way to the edge of the enemy's camp. Following Gideon's lead they blew their trumpets, smashed their jars and raised their torches. Then they shouted, "For the Lord and for Gideon".

The enemy heard the trumpets and then they heard the loud shattering sounds. They quickly woke up to find that their camp was surrounded by an army with burning torches, shouting out the victory of their God. The enemy must have thought that a mighty army of unknown thousands had them all surrounded because the Bible tells us that the enemy was so afraid and disoriented that they literally turned on each other and fought against themselves. The armies of Midian and Amelek then fled in fear from the Israelites. Gideon and His Men did not even have to lift a sword upon the camp.

-Selecting the Remnant-

You may be asking yourself what does three hundred fighting men turned theatrical performers have to do with our priestly call. Well, I believe that the system that God used when He selected Gideon's remnant, is similar to the method God will employ to choose His priests in our day. Let's take a closer look and see what these similarities might be.

First of all any man in Gideon's army who was afraid of the combat ahead was commanded to leave.

What type of fear makes men afraid to go into battle? The main trepidation would be the fear of death. There are almost always casualties in every battle. As a soldier you are not guaranteed that you will come back alive. But a good warrior must be willing to take that risk. As priest we can not be afraid of death either. As we have already learned in an earlier chapter, we must be willing to die to ourselves and to our agendas if we are to be chosen as priests before the glory of God.

As modern day priests, we must not allow the spirit of fear to rob us of our call. There are several types of fear that the enemy tries to ensnare us with. Probably the number one fear that the enemy is throwing at the people of God today is the fear of man. The enemy has us so concerned about what man will think that we have lost sight of what God thinks. We must never allow our call to be derailed by the fear of man.

The fear of man encompasses many other fears as well. The fear of failure, the fear of humiliation, and the fear of confrontation are all rooted in the fear of man. As priests we must not let fear rule us. We must combat fear with faith. Faith has the power to demolish all the fears in our lives.

The twenty-three thousand men who left Gideon's army because of their fear missed out on one of Israel's greatest victories. Fear robbed them of an opportunity to advance into an enormous destiny.

In the earth today spiritual battles are being fought all the time. Unfortunately, only a small remnant of believers is actually willing to go to the front lines and face the enemy head on. As priests we must be front liners. We must be willing to take a risk even if it looks impossible in the natural. I believe that the Lord is gathering together a remnant of priests who will be radical front liners for the Kingdom of God.

The next cut of Gideon's men took place at the river. Ten thousand men came to the river to drink. Those who put their face in the river were sent home but those who drew the water up to their mouths with their hands were kept.

When you kneel down and put your face in the water you can't see what is going on around you, but when you draw the water up to your mouth with your hands then you are able to keep an eye out for danger.

As carriers of God's glory we must be watchmen. Watchmen see what is coming before it gets here. It is difficult to sneak up on a skilled watchman because he will be aware of you long before you are even aware of him. Watchmen protect the city by forewarning the inhabitants of that city of any advancing threat. If a watchman is not paying attention then the enemy can sneak right into the city unaware. In Isaiah 56:10 we read about blind watchmen who are too busy sleeping to see what is coming. As priests we must be alert constantly watching for what is before us.

Watchmen not only see the enemy coming and alert the city of a present danger, they also see the messengers coming as well. The Lord is constantly moving in the area of the prophetic; He is persistently sending messages of instruction and encouragement to His people. God has chosen to use prophetic messengers to deliver His Kairos Word. As priests we must be prophetically watching for the directions and instructions that God wants to release to us.

After God selected the remnant army of Gideon, He gave them the most ridiculous battle plan that they had ever heard of. How was a torch, a jar and a trumpet supposed to defeat a vast army of countless thousands? God called the remnant not only to do the impossible but to also do it in an entirely unconventional way.

-Trusting God's Unusual Methods-

Sometimes God's plans seem ridiculous in our eyes. In scripture we find example after example where God used outlandish things to baffle the mindsets of men. The scriptures are full of examples where the ridiculous brought about the miraculous. As was mentioned in an earlier chapter, often God will call us to do the foolish things in order to accomplish His plan. God is continually challenging our paradigms. He wants us to think outside the box. In order to walk in the fullness of what God has for us we must break out of small thinking.

God's plan for our generation is for His children to move in His power in an unprecedented way. I tell you the truth, the miraculous movement ahead will not fit into your paradigm. You may as well get ready to have your mindset altered, because the coming outpouring of God's glory will usher in signs and wonders that the world has not yet seen.

I don't know about you, but I want more than anything to be a priest before the glory of God. I want to be one of those who stand by night in the house of the Lord and behold His glory. Yes, there is a preparation that must take place in my life in order for me to be chosen as one of the remnant, but I am more than willing to embrace it.

I believe that God will use a remnant again in our day. God is looking for some representatives who will answer the call to priesthood. The size of that remnant is yet to be decided. God may choose a few hundred people or He may choose several million. But there will be a remnant of priests. This remnant will carry a fore-runner anointing and God will use them to set in order the chosen places and the chosen people for His glory.

I believe that God is presently assembling this remnant. He is stripping off their old garments and washing them with His word. He is re-clothing them in new priestly garments. He is adding to them new levels of authority, anointings and giftings. He is realigning them and networking them together. This remnant will not be afraid to pay the price. In fact they will count it all as joy because of the reward that is set before them as they minister before the glory of God.

Anyone who has been a part of a remnant will testify of the overwhelming feeling of being outnumbered. They have often gazed at their small band of brothers and then looked at the task that they were attempting to accomplish and wondered how they would ever get the job done. Gideon's Men must have really wondered about their chances. Was it actually possible for 300 men to defeat an army of countless thousands? Yet in spite of the odds that they were faced with, they went for it anyway. Why, because they believed the Word of the Lord. They believed that 300 men plus one Almighty God could easily defeat the enemy's vast army.

As a remnant of priests, we will face obstacles that seem unsurpassable. Many of them will come from within the church. Many Christians, even church leaders, will simply decide not to receive the proposal that God wants to pour out His glory on the earth. Yet regardless of the obstacles, we must be willing to embrace the approaching move of God.

Are you one of them? Does your heart burn for more of God's glory? Are you willing to allow God to strip you and wash you so that He can clothe you in His priestly garments? If so, then I believe that God could be calling you to join the remnant of priests. God's perfect destiny is knocking on your hearts door.

Matthew 20 tells us that many are called but few are chosen. How do we transfer from one who is called to one who is chosen? First of all, respond to the call. Many are called, but only those who answer the priestly call will be chosen to fulfill the call.

Second, allow God to prepare you. God will require some changes in your life. These changes are essential if He is to fashion you into a priest before the His glory. Do not resist the preparation of the Lord. Let God have His way.

Third, be a person of faith, not a person of fear. Do not allow fear to keep you back from the destiny God has for you. Resist the spirit of fear in the name of Jesus Christ. As you do, you will see fear melt away and you will see God replacing that fear with new measures of faith.

And lastly, go for it. Walk in the fullness of what God has called you to. Put action to your faith and expect God's favor in your life.

I believe that the Lord is in the recruiting business. God wants more than anything to recruit you to join the remnant of priests. He is looking for a few good men and women. Are you willing to join the ranks of God's priestly remnant? Will you answer the call?

Chapter Fifteen

The Cry for Glory

Deep is Calling Out Unto Deep

There is a new sound rising up from the earth. If you listen you can hear it everywhere you go. In churches across the nation this sound is being lifted up. In prayer closets and home groups you can hear this new sound. Songs are being written in an attempt to express it. Intercessors are gathering together for the purpose of conveying it. Even the prophets are making proclamations regarding it. Deep is crying out unto deep. It is the cry of the redeemed for the Glory of God. It will be like nothing we have ever heard or witnessed before.

During the three years I lived in Colorado Springs, our church, Springs Harvest Fellowship, has actively pursued the Lord for His Glory. There was rarely a service that went by without a desperate cry going up for God's glory. Here in Madison, South Dakota, we too are calling out for the glory of God. We are anticipating a glory well here in our community that will radically touch and change the Midwest region of the United States. We do not see this as extreme. We believe that God chooses "whosoever will" to accomplish His purposes.

As I have visited other churches and have spoken to people from around the nation, I discover that we are not alone in this cry. Many fellowships are actively petitioning Heaven for the next outpouring of His glory upon the earth.

The Word tells us that God hears the cry of His people, and God's ear is bent toward His Church. He has heard our petition for His glory. Not only has He heard our cry, but I believe that He is the one that has put that cry in our hearts.

-Please Lord, Show Me Your Glory-

As we study the scriptures we find that we are not the first generation to cry out for the glory of God. A frustrated Moses climbed up Mount Sinai with a desire burning deep inside his heart. He had seen the hand of God on numerous occasions, but now he wanted to see something more. He had witnessed a burning bush; he had observed God's awesome power as the Lord unleashed the seven plagues upon Egypt; and he had stood on the shore and watched as the breath of God parted the Red Sea; yet here he was, still longing for something more. He had seen God's hand, but now he wanted to see His face. He longed to behold the glory of The Lord.

Exodus 33:18 says:

"And Moses said; please show me your glory." (NKJV)

Just as Moses cried out for the glory of God; so we too must cry out. We need to have the same passion for God's face that Moses had. It is no longer enough to just see the hand of God, we must desire His glory.

There is a key here that is vital as we petition the Lord for more of His glory. The key is this; Moses wanted to see the face of God. He did not just want to see God's glory; He wanted to see God Himself. In order for us to receive the glory of God we must not seek after the glory but the Glory Giver. If we are just after the glory of God, than we are seeking His hand and not His face. It is when we seek after the God of glory that we will find the glory of God.

-Revelation Accompanies His Glory-

God told Moses that he could not see His face and live, but God made a way for Moses to still see His glory. He allowed him to see His backside. He told Moses to hide himself in a cleft in the rock on the side of a mountain and then God placed His hand over Moses and shielded Him as He walked by. After God had passed by, He removed His hand and allowed Moses to see His back.

Moses then spent 40 days and 40 nights on the mountain with the Lord while God downloaded His truth and His laws. Revelation accompanied the exposure of God's glory. Many scholars believe that it was during this event that God gave Moses the divine understanding and insight to write the Pentateuch. Moses had seen the backside of God, and in doing so, he had seen the history of both God and Man. Moses would leave the mountain forty days later with new revelation of all that God had done since the foundations of the earth. Revelation accompanies the exposure of God's glory.

Another Biblical Example of Revelation accompanying God's Glory is found in the book of Revelation itself. Before the Lord downloaded the mysteries of the end times to John, He first took John to the throne room, where John came face to face with the magnificent Glory of God. It was after this encounter with God's glory that John was then given the Book of Revelation.

We are living in an exciting time. Once again a cry is rising in the midst of the people of God. We are petitioning the heavens for a new outpouring of God's glory. I know that very soon that petition will be answered by God Himself. He is about to reveal His glory upon the earth, and once again new revelation from the Father will accompany the glory of God. We are about to come to know the goodness of our God in ways that we have never known it before, because His glory will bring fresh revelation.

Isaiah 60:1 says:

"Arise; shine; for your light has come! And the glory of the Lord is risen upon you." (NKJV)

These are the days when the glory of God will indeed arise upon His Bride. We are about to embark on some of the most thrilling days our generation will ever see. But the question is, Are we ready? And if not, how do we get ready?

First of all, we must answer the priestly call as we have already learned. Regardless of the cost we must be willing to become a holy priesthood unto the Lord. We must embrace the price tag of sacrifice that comes with this great call. We must allow Him to prepare us for the ministry ahead.

Second, we must prepare a place for His glory. Just like in Solomon's temple, all the pieces must be in place. We need to ask the Lord what those pieces are. We need to seek the Lord for the right ingredients to the divine recipe for His glory. He is indeed rebuilding David's fallen tent. The visible manifestation of the Lord's Shekinah will rest once again upon the people of God. We must embrace the supernatural so that it can be displayed through us in extraordinary measure.

Third, as we prepare a place for His glory, we must allow His drill to dig. We must allow him to shake our current structures and see what has been built by God and what has been built by man. We also must allow His drill to unearth everything that needs to be unearthed. Those things that we have buried deep within us are the very things that He wants to deal with and set us free from. We also must let His drill push holes straight through our agendas. Our motto must be: His will before my will and His agenda before my agenda.

Fourth, we must prepare for the harvest that is to come. Our focus must get off the church and its programs and get on the lost and their need of a Savior. We need to have a plan to not only get them saved but also to get them rooted and discipled in the things of the Lord. Our focus must be outward not inward. We must return to our primary purpose as followers of Christ; the great commission.

And lastly, we must cry out for His glory. God will answer us when we cry out to Him. Not only will He answer, but He will show us great and mighty things.

Jeremiah 33:3 says,

"Call to Me, and I will answer you, and show you great and mighty things, which you do not know."(NKJV)

God is about to show His glory to His people; our present job is to cry out for it. He will reveal His power in the earth and the whole earth will know it.

Habakkuk 2:14 says

"For the earth will be filled with the knowledge of the glory of the LORD, as the waters cover the sea."(NIV)

In the past, we have been the ones asking all the questions. We are constantly petitioning the Lord, and asking Him to move on our behalf. But now the tables are turning. Now, I believe that it is the Lord who is asking the questions, and He is very specific in what He is asking. God is not looking for those who simply know the right answers; He is looking for those who will begin to implement what they know. These are some of the questions that I believe the Lord is asking us:

Do you hunger for Me?

Are you desperate for My Glory?

Are you desperate enough to cry out for it?

Can you relate to the cry of Moses?

Are you no longer satisfied with just seeing My hand?

Do you long to see My face?

Are you tired of simply living on yesterday's outpourings?

If you answered yes to these questions then you are exactly where you need to be. Yes, it is a frustrating place. Desperation isn't fun. But it is in that place of desperation where we begin to cry out for more on the Lord. God promises in the book of Jeremiah that He will answer us when we call.

It is time for our hearts to come into agreement with the heart of God. We already know that the desire of God's heart is to re-establish His weighty Kabod and manifest His Shekinah upon the earth. Now is the time for us to become as passionate for His outpouring as God is to pour it out.

Will you join this holy priesthood? Will you join with the thousands of others that are being raised up in this day to carry the glory of God? You have a choice before you. Will you let Him ignite your heart for His glory? Will you allow Him to overshadow you with His Kabod so that He can deposit His Shekinah within you? These are the questions that God is asking. What will your answers be?

CPSIA information can be obtained at www.ICGtesting.com
Printed in the USA
LVOW08s1949150114

369511LV00001B/7/A